You may find
this interesting
Regards, Simon

VIETNAM SETTLEMENT: WHY 1973, NOT 1969?

*First in the seventh series of Rational Debate Seminars
sponsored by the American Enterprise Institute
held at
American Enterprise Institute
Washington, D. C.*

ROBERT GORALSKI
Moderator

VIETNAM SETTLEMENT: WHY 1973, NOT 1969?

Morton A. Kaplan • Abram Chayes
G. Warren Nutter • Paul C. Warnke
John P. Roche • Clayton Fritchey

RATIONAL DEBATE SERIES

American Enterprise Institute for Public Policy Research
Washington, D. C.

ISBN 0-8447-2038-0
Library of Congress Catalog Card Number L.C. 73-84466

FOREWORD

This book presents a three-part discussion on the issue of why the Vietnam War was settled in 1973 rather than 1969. Originally televised on three evenings in February, this debate is the twenty-fourth in AEI's continuing series of Rational Debates. It features indictment and defense of the Vietnam policy pursued during President Nixon's first term, as well as searching appraisal of the Southeast Asia policies of the Kennedy and Johnson years. From the differing viewpoints of the academic community, high government service, and journalism, the benefits and costs of prolonging American military involvement in Vietnam for the four years January 1969 through January 1973 are explored.

Among the questions considered are: Have the additional four years been worth the lives lost, dollars spent, and domestic tranquillity upset? Is South Vietnam now appreciably better off, from both American and Vietnamese standpoints? What are the relative merits of the policies of the Nixon administration and its predecessors in Indochina? What kind of peace could the United States have hoped for in 1969? What kind of settlement did it gain in 1973?

In a free society, public attitudes are crucial in public policy formation. They significantly influence the options open to public officials, whether elected or appointed. It is vital, therefore, that thought leaders who help form public attitudes have available the results of innovative thought from as wide a range of sources as possible. We believe that this volume will make an important contribution to this end.

July 1973

William J. Baroody

President

American Enterprise Institute

for Public Policy Research

CONTENTS

PART ONE

Two Academic Views

PART TWO

Two Insiders' Views

PART THREE

Two Journalists' Views

PART ONE
Two Academic Views

LECTURES

MORTON A. KAPLAN

We have two questions before us. Could President Nixon have ended the war in Vietnam on essentially the same terms in 1969 that he achieved in 1973? If he could have done so, would the consequences have been the same?

With respect to the first question, until very recently, the North Vietnamese were asking us essentially to present them with the South on a silver platter. I refer here not so much to the public demands of the North Vietnamese as to their inflexibility in the private negotiating sessions. They were demanding that we force President Thieu out of power, impose a coalition government, and remove ourselves in a way that would have destroyed our remaining credibility as well as that of those South Vietnamese who had cooperated with us. The crushing impact such a settlement would have had upon South Vietnamese politics and psychology would have utterly destroyed the prospect for survival of a non-Communist South Vietnam.

The first indication I had that the Communists were interested in any serious negotiation came in April 1972 during the beginning of the spring offensive. Information that I received from a reliable source implied strongly that President Thieu's removal was no longer on the Communist agenda. Although this was denied by a diplomatic source, it was obvious that there was a linkage between that offensive and the push for a settlement. It was also obvious that the Russians at last had an incentive to bring pressure to bear upon the North Vietnamese to negotiate a compromise peace. When I told a friend on the National Security Council that Thieu's status might no longer be at issue, he was quite surprised, thus indicating that this information had not yet reached, or at least had not yet circulated throughout, the National Security Council.

The public sequence of events was educational. Henry Kissinger traveled to Moscow and then almost immediately resumed the private talks with the North Vietnamese in Paris. The resumption of these talks appeared related to information received in Moscow. However, the talks were quickly terminated with a public display of irritation by Mr. Kissinger. It turned out that the North Vietnamese had technically kept to the indicated terms, but had done this in a way that made a mockery of the negotiations. They were still demanding that the United States bring down the South Vietnamese government for them. Thus, despite the pressures from Moscow, and also from Peking, the North Vietnamese still proved inflexible. It remained impossible to discuss, let alone to agree upon, a compromise that reflected the battle-field conditions. All efforts in the private negotiations to do this met the same firm rebuff they had met since the inception of discussions in 1968.

Toward the end of the spring, I was in touch with another extremely knowledgeable person. I expressed the opinion that the offensive had been intended as a prelude to a settlement. With the Viet Cong force extremely weak in the

South, an invasion from the North was necessary to produce the type of territorial control that would enable them to risk a settlement. However, in Paris, contrary to Russian expectations, the North Vietnamese had not displayed the flexibility they had promised and were still negotiating on the old unacceptable terms that had consistently frustrated successful negotiations. Information from other independent sources had indicated Russian anger with the North Vietnamese. In the context of the information I had, this indicated a double-cross of the Russians by the North Vietnamese. However, my interlocutor indicated that the Russians still hoped, particularly given the failure of the offensive, that the North Vietnamese would finally agree to settle along the indicated terms but perhaps only at the very last minute, thus implying that they would do so just before the elections.

This was shrewd analysis. The North Vietnamese had forced one President out of office by refusing to negotiate except on terms unacceptable to him. They had attempted the same game with a second President. Turmoil in the universities, vitriolic opposition in the Senate, slanted news on radio and television, and an intellectual chorus of opposition to the war gave them every reason to believe that they would succeed. However, the President's handling of the situation restored some public support for his policies, his Vietnamization policy restored some strength to the South Vietnamese government, and the election campaign demonstrated the fatuousness of his opponent. Even the North Vietnamese soon realized that the elections held no solace for them and that they would be faced with four more years of Richard Nixon. On the other hand, their bargaining influence would be greatest just before the elections and weakened just after it. This provided the obvious incentive for their presentation of a serious proposal toward the close of the presidential campaign.

However, we do not really require such anecdotal information. The facts are clearly on the public record. Four years of successful diplomacy by the Nixon administration created a political climate in which both the Soviet Union and Communist China had strong incentives to bring pressure to bear upon the North Vietnamese to accept a negotiated settlement that did not destroy the South Vietnamese government or humiliate the United States.

This diplomacy was foreshadowed in statements made by Richard Nixon even before he became President. His 1968 article in *Foreign Affairs* indicated a desire for a rapprochement with Communist China, and statements subsequent to the inauguration reinforced this posture. Yet, the readjustments were not easy. Although 1969 was the year of greatest Russian pressure on China—including hints of nuclear attack—it was to take two years before the Chinese responded to Richard Nixon's overtures. The internal politics of China are murky and we cannot be certain of the reasons for the delay. Among other possible reasons, there was apparently strong internal resistance to the American opening. Some believe that the Lin Piao affair was related to this resistance. In any event, the inauguration of ping-pong diplomacy by Chou En-lai in 1971 began the process of détente. By then the Chinese had opted for an American connection rather than seeking reassurance through concessions to the Soviet Union and, therefore, they had an incentive to help avoid a humiliating defeat for the United States. More than this, they required an American presence in Southeast Asia to offset the Soviet Union and a continued American presence in Western Europe to complicate any Russian considerations of harsh pressure—or even a nuclear strike—against themselves.

On the other hand, the Chinese opening to the United States produced fear in the Soviet Union. By the end of 1971 Russian suspicions were so great that the American-Soviet détente might have been jeopardized. It was necessary for the Nixon administration, in a display of diplomatic flexibility, to limit its connection with China in a way that did not worry the Chinese but did inhibit Soviet fears of a Chinese-American alliance. As part of this process, the United States continued to engage in measures of détente with the Soviet Union, including successful strategic arms limitation treaty (SALT) negotiations. This ensured the Soviet Union of a relatively coequal role with the United States in world politics—an outcome of great importance to the Soviet leadership. Economic pressures and the desire not to drive the United States into the feared Chinese-American alliance gave the Soviet Union an incentive to help arrange a peace in South Vietnam. For the first time, both China and Russia had more of an incentive to assist the United States than to struggle over comparative influence within North Vietnam, although this last consideration continued to play a minor role in their policies toward that area.

Yet this dénouement was not an automatic response to world politics. A weaker American posture in Western Europe, as proposed by some, might have encouraged the Soviet Union to solve its problems by Finlandization of

Western Europe. A scuttling of the American position in South Vietnam might have convinced the Chinese of the unreliability of an American connection and have strengthened those forces in China seeking safety through concessions to the Soviet Union. Careful balance was required or the entire basis of American security in both Europe and Asia would have been threatened. Thus, rather than being the result of inevitable tendencies in world politics, the diplomacy of the Nixon administration created the temporary stability that we now enjoy.

Even if we were to assume—contrary to the facts—that the same agreement reached in January 1973 could have been reached in 1969, the consequences of the agreement would have been far different at that time. The situation in 1969 was the product of the decisions that had been made in the previous eight years. The Kennedy administration had fooled itself into believing that it was winning a guerrilla war. It was never able to bring itself either to a decision to pull out before a genuine American commitment had been made or to conduct the war in a way that provided some prospect of succeeding at a modest cost. During South Vietnamese President Diem's great political weakness in the summer of 1961, the administration refrained from pressing the political reforms upon him that might have restored the viability of the South Vietnamese government. It forced him into a resettlement program copied from Malaya but unsuited to Vietnamese conditions. It finally agreed to his being brought down so that we could win the war, but then discovered that it did not know what to do with Vietnam after his removal. I know of no more decisive commitment a nation can make than to bring down the president of a friendly country in order to win a war.

In the absence of an organized machinery of government in South Vietnam, and with the rapid circulation of governments after the coup, the situation deteriorated. Under the tutelage of the finest brains the Kennedy establishment had to offer, the U.S. then moved in bodily, thrusting aside the South Vietnamese army. Secretary of Defense Robert McNamara took the war over, reserving its conduct to the United States and consigning only inadequate and out-of-date equipment to the South Vietnamese army (ARVN). We then engaged in the nonsense of search and destroy, laying waste huge tracts of the countryside, only to discover that the enemy had withdrawn from our path and infiltrated back as we continued to advance. With our bombing and artillery strikes, we created recruits for the Viet Cong while failing to engage extensively in the police, paramilitary and counterinsurgency tactics that might have held territory and controlled population if we had moved more slowly and carefully. If the overthrow of the Diem regime had constituted a massive American commitment to Vietnam, the policies pursued by the United States subsequent to that overthrow reinforced our commitment beyond the legitimate doubts of a moral person. So much damage was done to Vietnam—to its ecology, to its economy, and to its people—as a result of American military and political actions that we had reached one of those rare episodes in the history of nations in which one nation acquires a moral veto on the actions of another. If the Vietnamese had wished us to withdraw, we would have had no option but to do so. On the other hand, if they wished us to remain, we had no right simply to withdraw.

If we had any doubts as to where the Vietnamese people stood on this issue, they should have disappeared during the 1972 spring offensive. No population movements were observed toward the Communist lines. Although not all people fleeing the Communist advance were partisans of the South Vietnamese government, the massiveness and direction of the refugees is at least worth noting. More than this, however, there were no uprisings against the South Vietnamese government during this period of weakness. This was not a consequence of the repressive efficiency of the government, for it was far less efficient in this respect than the Diem regime that had not been able to prevent the Buddhist uprisings in 1963. Nor could it be attributed to the efficiency of its police, for jails had been more packed under Diem and the actions of the political police more suspect. Even the An Quang Buddhists, despite their strong opposition to the Thieu regime, kept their supporters from engaging in any actions that might have led to a precipitate American withdrawal. The message of the South Vietnamese people was loud and clear. It could be missed only by those who were determined to believe otherwise, regardless of the evidence.

We had massive power and spent massive amounts of money. We could have paved the entire country in concrete if we had made the effort. By 1968 one of the most brutal, expensive, and stupid politico/military efforts the world has ever seen had finally, through sheer preponderance of resources, reached the point where success was in sight. With support from the public, a more sensible policy on the part of the United States could have reassured beyond question the preservation of a non-Communist government in South Vietnam.

Shrewd as always, the North Vietnamese employed psychological warfare against us. They struck in a Tet offensive that was a military disaster for them but that finally cracked the will of those members of the administration who feared B– grades from the *New York Times*. Dissension within the administration and a desire for popularity with students on the part of famous academicians helped reinforce a crisis of legitimacy that stemmed more from the desire of young people to escape military service than from any other motive. The subsiding of the crisis of legitimacy coincided with the virtual ending of the draft, resoluteness on the part of the President, and a restoration of authority within the universities. Our young people, goaded by insecurity and fearful of their future, had tested their elders and found them wanting. They discovered indecision, lack of conviction, and attempts to curry favor. The frenzy increased. When their fears were diminished and when the authorities behaved with greater conviction and resoluteness, the crisis passed. On the other hand, if the intellectual establishment had had its way, the crisis of legitimacy on the left of the political spectrum would have increased until a firm reaction on the right would have crushed it with a display of might that would have been a genuine threat to the liberal values of our democracy. A policy of "scuttling" in Vietnam might well have played a role in provoking such a crisis of legitimacy. Fortunately for the United States, at the vital moment it found firm leadership in the nation and in at least some of the universities.

Nonetheless a virtual military victory was turned into a political defeat. A decent man was forced out of the American presidency because his party turned on him and because his administration had been run by those very officials who had made all the mistakes to begin with. Having brought the war almost to the point of military victory, they panicked and sought defeat. Their desertion of our men in uniform helped to destroy the morale of our armed forces. By agreeing that the war was a "dirty" war, they destroyed the value of military service for all those in arms and stole from our black soldiers their pride in themselves and their claim upon a grateful nation for recognition of their elementary, political, social, and economic rights. In the process, the Democratic party of Franklin Roosevelt, Harry Truman, Adlai Stevenson, and Lyndon Johnson was captured by an unrepresentative elite—an event that bore its final fruits in the election of 1972.

By 1969, the ARVN, the Viet Cong, and much of the North Vietnamese army had been destroyed in the course of the war. Even if one could have got the same terms in 1969 that President Nixon received in 1973, they would have left South Vietnam incapable of defending itself either from external or internal attack—unless there were guarantees against further interference by the North in the South's affairs. The rebuilding of the ARVN was not something that could take place overnight. Moreover, it had to be carried out at a time when the credibility of the United States was diminished because of the unwillingness of the United States to support an American armed presence in Vietnam. Extrication with honor required good nerves, cool intelligence, and a respect for the potential independence of the South Vietnamese. That this could be substantially accomplished within a short period of four years during which American forces were being withdrawn is a comment on the previous eight years. The timing is still somewhat risky, however, and we probably would have got still better terms if we had had more support at home.

Even the delay between October and January was essential. If the agreement had been imposed in October, quite apart from substantive differences in the terms reached in January from those proposed in October, it would have appeared to have been a total American imposition on President Thieu. The intervening three months gave him time to react and to adjust. The concessions allowed him to demonstrate at least a minimum of independence from the United States and of control over the decision. This was essential to some restoration of his authority.

Whether or not the present agreement is the best that could have been reached is open to question. It is substantially better than any agreement that could have been reached through early 1972. That the South Vietnamese have a reasonable opportunity to maintain their independence and to resist totalitarian rule is a remarkable outcome. In this respect, criticism of the Thieu regime as oppressive and authoritarian is disgraceful. Habeas corpus was eliminated by President Lincoln during the Civil War. In Great Britain during the Second World War, many individuals were seized under the Crown Acts without charges and incarcerated for the entire period of the war. South Vietnam did not have the advantage either of a democratic tradition or a functioning democratic system. It had passed through roughly seventy years of French colonial rule. It was then occupied by the Japanese during the Second World War. After 1945, it was in almost constant turmoil from a civil war. That there are opposition parties and that they have done well in elections is remarkable. Controls on the press are less remarkable than the fact that an opposition press exists. Yes, the regime is repressive and it exercises some powers ordinarily thought of as authoritarian. Given the conditions it faces, however, any objective person would be far more impressed with the degree of freedom and the right to political opposition that continue to exist in that unhappy country. Many who rant against the Thieu regime make pilgrimages to the totalitarian Hanoi regime and find praise for the dictatorial Yugoslav regime.

The continued viability of the South Vietnamese regime and the fact that it has a reasonable opportunity to maintain its independence is even more remarkable, given a U.S. presidential campaign during which the Democratic party's candidate proudly announced that if he were elected, President Thieu would flee the country. Several days later, he noted that since President Thieu had been our ally, he would offer him asylum in Miami. Suppose—in a similar conflict in the Middle East—he had said that if he were President, Golda Meir and Moshe Dayan would flee their country and he would offer them asylum in Miami, or perhaps in the Catskills.

There was a moral issue in Vietnam—an overriding one. Although I shall refrain from any such statements as "the most of anything in American history," the attempt to force the surrender of the South Vietnamese was one of the most outrageous political developments I have witnessed in my lifetime. Yet this proposal was supported by those very former officials who mired us in Vietnam, who destroyed the South Vietnamese army, who retreated in the face of victory, who have been wrong in every crucial decision of that entire tragic episode, who wanted "in" when they should have wanted "out" and who wanted "out" when they should have wanted "in."

There is much in the world that is doubtful, including most of the decisions concerning Vietnam. But the two questions I started with—could the war have been ended in 1969 on approximately the same terms, and would the consequences have been the same—seem to be among the few questions that have clear, and negative, answers.

ABRAM CHAYES

The President has remarked that some of the strongest opponents of the war in Vietnam seem to be the least enthusiastic about the peace. Let me state at the beginning that I welcome the peace agreement with the deepest gratitude. I think the President and his advisers are thoroughly sincere in their hopes that the agreement will function effectively and in their commitment to carry it out on our part. And in my view there is every reason to expect that the agreement will, in fact, lead to the termination of United States military involvement in Indochina, whatever may be the fate of Vietnam itself.

Moreover, any discussion of the war policy of the past four years must recognize that on January 21, 1969, President

15

Nixon inherited a full-fledged war in being, a war that, whatever his views about it, was not of his own making. As he said in his first address to the nation on this subject in May 1969, he no longer had the choice of not intervening.[1] That bridge had been crossed.

But wholehearted gratitude and relief that peace has finally come need not and should not foreclose careful study and analysis of any part of the war policy, including the past four years.

The central issues raised by the war for the American polity are the uses and the limits of military force in today's world. And, at least the first step in coming to conclusions on those very fundamental questions is to look as objectively and dispassionately as we can at the gains and the costs of these last four years of war. And we must make the effort to compare costs with benefits, to match means against ends.

Many of the physical costs of these last four years of war can be measured with some precision. Some of them are illustrated graphically in the accompanying charts.

First, the cost in dollars: Budgeted expenditures for the Vietnam War, 1969-72, came to $62 billion, just under half the total of dollar expenditures on the war.

Another physical dimension, the cost in air and ground ammunition fired into Vietnam, North and South: the 1969-72 total is 7.6 million tons, well over half of the ordnance expended in the entire war.

The third chart deals with the human cost of the last four years. It quantifies an enormity of human anguish:

---

[1] May 15, 1969, p. 16.

Figure 1
BUDGETED EXPENDITURES
FOR THE VIETNAM WAR

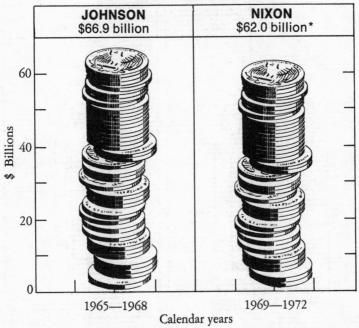

* Includes expenditures through June 30, 1972.
Note: For the difference between budgeted and incremental expendi-
tures, see Mr. Kaplan's rebuttal, Table 1.
Source: "A Statistical Fact Sheet on the Indochina War," Indochina
Resource Center, Washington, D. C., September 27, 1972.

More than 15,000 Americans were killed, more than
100,000 wounded.

Our South Vietnamese allies suffered military casualties
of almost 100,000 deaths and almost 300,000 wounded,
and civilian casualties of 165,000 killed and over 400,000
wounded.

17

Figure 2
MUNITIONS EXPENDED
IN VIETNAM WAR—GROUND AND AIR

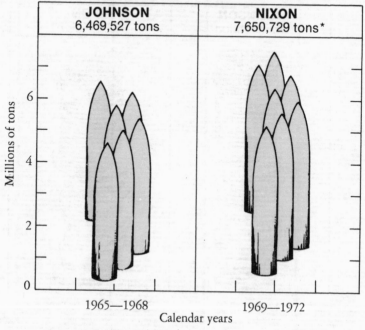

JOHNSON 6,469,527 tons	NIXON 7,650,729 tons*

Millions of tons

1965—1968   1969—1972

Calendar years

*Includes air munitions through August 31, 1972 and ground munitions through June 30, 1972.
Source: See Figure 1.

As to the North Vietnamese, the Department of Defense reports about 440,000 military deaths. We have no official figures as to wounded, but based on DOD's estimate of 1.5 wounded per death (compared to the 3-to-1 ratio of the South Vietnamese military), the figure works out to 660,000. There are no figures on North Vietnamese civilian casualties.

And then there are the refugees—people, families uprooted from their homes, their land, their villages, to

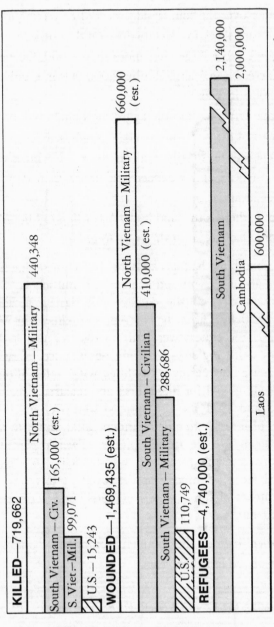

Figure 3

HUMAN COST OF VIETNAM WAR (EXCLUDING NORTH VIETNAMESE CIVILIANS)
January 1969—September 1972

KILLED—719,662

North Vietnam — Military 440,348

South Vietnam — Civ. 165,000 (est.)

S. Viet.— Mil. 99,071

U.S. — 15,243

WOUNDED—1,469,435 (est.)

North Vietnam — Military 660,000 (est.)

South Vietnam — Civilian 410,000 (est.)

South Vietnam — Military 288,686

U.S. 110,749

REFUGEES—4,740,000 (est.)

South Vietnam 2,140,000

Cambodia 2,000,000

Laos 600,000

Note: U.S. figures include casualties through September 9, 1972 (excluding deaths in nonhostile activities). Other figures are inclusive through July 31, 1972.
Source: See Figure 1.

wander over the countryside, most often ending in a tin or cardboard shack in a shanty town on the outskirts of Saigon or some other large city: more than 2,000,000 new refugees created in Vietnam, plus 2,000,000 in Cambodia and 600,000 in Laos.

So that if we look at the aggregate human cost of the last four years of the war—human beings, whose lives were ended or wrenched drastically out of shape—it comes to over 2 million dead and wounded and more than 4½ million refugees in all.

Finally, there is the land itself. According to Eliot Marshall and Tom Geoghegan in the *New Republic:*

> U.S. bombing had pocked the Indochinese landscape with about 26 million craters, 21 million in South Vietnam alone ... the damage will last a decade or more: 10 years after the bombing of Okinawa in World War II the craters were still barren. Craters in Vietnam's delta region—occurring about once every 100 feet—are now permanently filled with water, affording a breeding pool for mosquitoes and malaria ... between 1962 and 1971 the U.S. sprayed well over six million acres of forest with a defoliant chemical meant to make the enemy visible to spy planes. Twenty percent of South Vietnam's forestland was treated ... 6.5 billion board feet of lumber was destroyed in this way, and ... patches of forest were completely and permanently wiped out.[2]

More than half of the total environmental damage is the product of the last four years.

---

[2] "Calculating the Costs," *New Republic,* February 10, 1973, p. 21.

I do not take the position that such an expenditure of blood and treasure can never be justified by the objectives pursued. But surely the weight of suffering that is represented in these numbers puts a very heavy burden of proof on one who would justify the policies that incurred these costs.

Over the past ten years, opponents of the war came increasingly to challenge the basic assumptions of the war policy.

They argued that the United States has no significant security interest in Indochina.

They insisted that the Thieu regime was not a worthy or even legitimate object of American concern. By any index it has been an authoritarian and repressive government. No political freedoms have existed in South Vietnam under Thieu—no free speech or press, no political opposition. Thousands upon thousands of political prisoners languish in cruel and inhuman confinement. Even after the cease-fire, American reporters, seeking to interview North Vietnamese truce supervision personnel on their arrival in the South, were threatened with arrest and expulsion from the country. Genuine political support for the regime, it is said, is thin or nonexistent, and Thieu has been maintained in power only by virtue of American arms and dollars. This is not to deny that North Vietnam is also a totalitarian dictatorship. Nor need we assert that the sole criterion for United States support should be the conformity of the recipient to the practices and mechanisms of western democracy. Still, the recognition of the Thieu regime for what it is—a shabby, corrupt and on the whole cruel dictatorship—is surely relevant to the propriety and scope of our commitment.

Opponents have urged, further, that any legitimate United States interest in a non-Communist South Vietnam could have been pursued through a coalition government, with at least as great a chance of success and with considerably less bloodshed. The 1962 Laos agreements included a coalition government, and, although the settlement did not hold, it did not prove to be the prelude to a Communist takeover either. And the recent agreement has reendorsed the 1962 Laos accords.

I share these views, but I shall not press them here. For purposes of this discussion, I shall accept the assumption of the administration that the survival of the Thieu regime is a "good thing" for the United States, and that a chance for it to survive was a valid object of United States policy. Indeed, the main virtue claimed for the settlement by its proponents is that it does give that regime "a chance" to survive as the government of South Vietnam.

But a defense of the war policy of the last four years, even on these assumptions must show, first, that this chance of survival is really substantial; and it must show, second, that no alternative course of action seemed reasonably likely to lead to the same outcome, at significantly smaller cost.

I believe the policy of the last four years fails on both counts.

First, what can be said of the reality of Thieu's chances for survival under the peace agreement? President Nixon, in May 1969, outlined the elements of a settlement that would provide such a chance. It "will require the withdrawal of all non-South Vietnamese forces from South Vietnam, and procedures for political choice that give each significant group in South Vietnam a real opportunity to participate in the political life of the nation." [3]

Almost four years later, on December 30, 1972, only three weeks before the settlement was announced, President Thieu, in his interview with Oriana Fallaci, was saying much the same thing, "Accepting the presence of North Vietnamese troops by juridical agreement, ratified by an international conference is absolutely unacceptable ... what kind of peace is a peace that gives the North Vietnamese the right to keep their troops here ... that legalizes their presence here *de facto*." [4]

But one essential feature of the settlement reached on January 25 is that it does not "require the withdrawal of all non-South Vietnamese forces," and it does "legalize the North Vietnamese presence *de facto*." Thus, one of the essential conditions necessary to give Thieu's government a reasonable chance, as specified by both President Nixon and General Thieu himself, has not been achieved.

What of the political capabilities of the Thieu government? In 1969, in answer to President Nixon's request after his inauguration for a thoroughgoing review of the situation in Vietnam, "the military community"—that is the secretary of defense, the joint chiefs of staff and the Saigon command—reported as follows: "As the government of Vietnam's major presence in the countryside, the RVNAF [Republic of Vietnam armed forces] as presently constituted will only continue

---

[3] *New York Times,* May 15, 1969, p. 16.

[4] *New Republic,* January 20, 1973, p. 17.

to widen the gap which exists between the Government and the rural population." [5]

Four years later, that prediction seems to be fulfilled. Frances FitzGerald, whose book, *Fire in the Lake,* has been almost universally acclaimed for its insight into the social structure and culture of Vietnam, says in a post-settlement article:

> The [Thieu government] ... is a product of the American pacification of Vietnam, a vast military administration, containing most of the draft age men, without a political direction, except the vague negative of anti-Communism.... It occupies the country rather than governs it. And ... the success of this occupation depends largely on the use of its great weaponry to keep the population concentrated in a few places and locked in a state of economic dependency on the United States.... [6]

The fighting qualities of this huge army were demonstrated last May, after three years of Vietnamization, when but for massive American air and sea support on an unprecedented scale, including the bombing of Hanoi and the mining of Haiphong Harbor, the North Vietnamese offensive would have overwhelmed the South's forces.

More broadly, we may ask, what chance can there be for a government that has presided over a war in which, all told, about 2 million people—one in every nine—were killed or wounded and in which some 8 million, almost half the pop-

---

[5] Excerpts from National Security memorandum, as reported in *New York Times,* April 26, 1972, p. 16.

[6] "Can the War End?" *New York Review of Books,* February 22, 1973, p. 13.

ulation, have been made refugees; where the economy has been shattered, the traditional way of life and social structure has been pulverized, and the land itself has been disastrously scarred. To quote Ms. FitzGerald again:

> After thirteen years of a major war, South Vietnam has become ungovernable—a mass of refugees, an ecological disaster, and a catalogue of social and economic ills. Those who rush—or are rushed—into taking responsibility for this anarchy are bound to be repudiated in the long run.[7]

As a matter of fact, General Thieu himself does not seem to rate the settlement too highly on this score. He has been even less enthusiastic about it than the American antiwar groups to whom President Nixon referred. It is generally acknowledged that he was brought to accept the agreement only by severe American pressure. And his compliance has been by no means unstinting.

Despite these deficiencies from the point of view of President Nixon's and General Thieu's objectives, the settlement represents something short of the maximum position of the North that the Thieu government should be replaced.

But assuming that this was a plus, the question remains whether a result similar to the 1973 settlement could have been reached by any alternative policy available to Richard M. Nixon when he took office in 1969. I believe there was such an alternative in 1969. It was the course of serious, intensive and sustained negotiations looking toward the kind of compromise that was ultimately reached. Such a negotiating program was urged by many at the time, including

---

[7] Ibid., p. 14.

outgoing Secretary of Defense Clark Clifford, Ambassador Averell Harriman, and others. Ambassador Harriman, indeed, believes the North Vietnamese were signalling their desire for such a settlement in a variety of ways. Whether *they* were or not, *we* did not give the negotiating route a serious and responsible try.

After the government-wide review of policy I referred to above, the President chose instead the route of Vietnamization, although the study indicated that this course would involve several more years of heavy fighting. At the same time, the President announced his demands for a settlement—withdrawal of all outside troops including the North Vietnamese, and agreement on internationally supervised elections thereafter to determine whether Thieu would continue to rule in the South. Although these proposals sounded good for domestic consumption in the United States, they were tantamount to a complete defeat for the North Vietnamese and the Viet Cong. These objectives could not be achieved by negotiation, only by military victory. And our government knew this. In fact, I do not believe they were ever intended as a basis for serious negotiations.

We persisted in this position for two and a half years—years which saw the war spread to Laos and Cambodia. Although once, in August 1971, it appears that the United States briefly tendered a withdrawal in exchange for the release of United States prisoners, this approach does not seem to have been vigorously pursued.

Not until October 1971 did the Nixon administration finally begin to abandon its pursuit of military victory. Then, President Nixon, formally, modified the demand for simultaneous withdrawal of U.S. and North Vietnamese troops. But his eight-point proposal put forward in the secret negotiations at that time still linked the end of the war to a political settlement based on elections and included an express recognition of the principle of withdrawal of North Vietnamese troops.

Finally, on May 8, 1972, after the outbreak of the North Vietnamese spring offensive, the President, in the speech announcing renewed bombing of the North, made what I believe to be the key concessions. He proposed a cease-fire in place, the return of United States prisoners, and withdrawal of United States forces within four months. Thereafter there would be negotiations and a political settlement between the Vietnamese themselves. There was no mention of North Vietnamese withdrawal. And there was no linkage of the end of the fighting and U.S. withdrawal to any form of political settlement.

These are essentially the terms of the final agreement. Although they were not accepted immediately by the other side, Dr. Kissinger's trans-Atlantic travel schedule picked up very quickly, and he made a number of journeys to Paris during the summer. Within six months—in early October, according to Dr. Kissinger—Hanoi and the Provisional Revolutionary Government had accepted the basic principle of separating the military and political aspects of the settlement. By the end of October an agreement had been reached that was in all essential elements the same as the one finally signed.

All sorts of military activity was occurring on both sides during this period—military action that created the havoc and destruction summarized in the charts. Many say that only this military activity convinced the North Vietnamese that they could not themselves win the victory. But tragically, it seems it was necessary also to convince the President that *he* could not win. Once he abandoned his two demands for North Vietnamese withdrawal and an agreed political settlement, the other side responded within a period that is reasonable by diplomatic standards.

No one can prove that this same response would have occurred if the President had offered his May 1972 terms in May 1969. But there was reason to think that it might. The ultimate settlement was not so different from the terms of the two earlier Indochina agreements in 1954 and 1962. Indeed, as early as 1965, North Vietnamese Premier Pham Van Dong announced a four-point position that sounds not too different from the settlement ultimately reached.[8]

Was it not the obligation of a great and responsible nation at least to have tested this course, before embarking itself and the Vietnamese people, North and South, on four years of the application of overwhelming and unprecedented military force in an effort to impose our will?

Much is said about the importance of demonstrating the validity and viability of America's commitments to its allies. But in the words of Alistair Buchan, a sympathetic observer of our plight, former director of the Institute of Strategic Studies and commandant of the Royal College of Defense Studies: "The greatest damage of the war has been to the

---

[8] See *Background Information Relating to Southeast Asia and Vietnam* (2d revised edition), Senate Committee on Foreign Relations, 89th Congress, 2d session (1966), p. 295.

international authority of the United States." [9] For Buchan and other friends of the United States in Europe, the Vietnam War raises grave questions about American judgment—our capacity to balance means and ends.

In my view, the erosion of the authority of the United States government goes much deeper than that. We are in the midst of a crisis of legitimacy, in which the capacity of the government to govern—to formulate and carry out policies at home and abroad—is gravely shaken. The crisis of legitimacy is the heritage of the Vietnam War. In a democracy there is no room for the principle that might makes right. Coercive power must be justified, legitimated by something larger than the desire to impose our own will.

Neither the Johnson nor the Nixon administrations accepted this essential obligation of a democratic government— the obligation of serious, principled justification of the war policy, entailing, as it did, immense destruction and suffering, here and in Vietnam. If this burden of justification had been accepted, I believe the policy would necessarily have changed. Since it was not, the legitimacy of the government itself is undermined. That is not attributable only to the last four years. But January 1969 was a potential turning point. The greatest cost of those years is an opportunity cost—the opportunity that was there in 1969 and lost—the opportunity to begin anew.

It will be a long time before we have such a chance again.

---

[9] *The London Observer,* January 28, 1973, p. 12.

REBUTTALS

MORTON A. KAPLAN

The University of Chicago was the first university in the country to restore the legitimacy of university administrations. It did this not by buckling under to the pressure of student demands but by finding an acceptable settlement to the situation at the university. We were the first to expel students. We were the first to call a halt to the uprisings that were occurring and that were encouraged by the weak responses of other administrations.

I think the United States would have had a serious legitimacy crisis if we had "bugged out" of Vietnam. That the crisis occurred because of the way in which we handled the war or even perhaps because of the way in which we got into it, I don't care to argue about. I accept that. But once we were in it, that crisis could not have been resolved by a bugout. I think students would have understood that one extremely well. In my view, the reason you see fewer riots in the cities today—the reason you see fewer disturbances all over—is that the present administration will not engage in that kind of weak behavior.

Now, with respect to whether the Thieu regime is repressive or authoritarian, as I recall, Abraham Lincoln engaged in certain repressive actions during the Civil War. And in the Second World War, the British government acting under the Crown Acts simply seized people and put them in jail.

31

In Vietnam we have a country that was under French colonial administration for 70 years, was occupied by the Japanese and has been at war for the last 30 or 35 years. The fact that there is a political opposition in South Vietnam at all, that there are some opposition papers which occasionally do come out, is indeed a remarkable achievement. This is far different from what occurs in the North.

Now, the regime is not enormously efficient. If there had been Buddhist riots during the April offensive, we wouldn't have had the agreement we have today. The An Quang Buddhists *didn't* riot, not because they were afraid of Thieu's repressive apparatus but precisely because they didn't want a Communist takeover.

It is true that the United States need never have gotten into this situation, that we don't have to solve every problem in the world regardless of the cost. But we have imposed tremendous penalties on the South Vietnamese in the last eight years. To bug out after that would be like the young man who "knocked up" a girl and, when asked if he was going to take care of the kid, said: No, I made a mistake—let's call a halt to the matter now. I don't think that would be responsible either.

My learned opponent has discussed the costs of the Vietnam War. The human costs seem to me the most important, and the Vietnamese people gave their answer dramatically on that issue. As to the monetary costs, Professor Chayes has presented a badly misleading picture of the Vietnam War outlays attributable to the Nixon administration. Among other things, his figures arbitrarily count half of the fiscal 1969 total within the Nixon years. That budget was Lyndon

Table 1

MILITARY OUTLAYS AND ESTIMATED COSTS OF SOUTHEAST ASIA WAR [a]

($ billions)

Fiscal year	Current Prices			Constant (FY 1973) Prices		
	Full war costs [b]	Incremental war costs [c]	Total military outlays	Full war costs [b]	Incremental war costs [c]	Total military outlays
1964	—	—	49.6	—	—	78.2
1965	.1	.1	45.7	.1	.1	70.9
1966	5.8	5.8	53.6	8.1	8.1	79.3
1967	20.1	18.4	66.5	26.7	24.6	95.0
1968	26.5	20.0	75.9	34.2	26.2	104.4
1969	28.8	21.5	76.2	35.5	27.0	100.3
1970	23.1	17.4	75.0	27.2	20.8	91.6
1971	14.7	11.5	72.2	16.5	13.0	82.9
1972 [d]	9.3	7.3	71.9	9.7	7.7	76.5
1973 [d]	7.1	5.8	72.8	7.1	5.8	72.8

[a] Excluding military retired pay.
[b] All costs incurred in the Vietnam theater or in support thereof.
[c] Costs (direct and support) of units not part of the baseline force and, for baseline force units, costs over and above normal peacetime operating costs.
[d] As revised in July 1972.

Johnson's. In my opinion, the best comparison would be between incremental costs in constant dollars for the four Johnson budgetary years (fiscal 1966 through fiscal 1969) and the four Nixon budgetary years (fiscal 1970 through fiscal 1973). Those figures are $85.6 billion and $47.3 billion, respectively. The year-by-year data in both current and constant dollars are illuminating as well. They are given on page 149 of "The Economics of Defense Spending: A Look at the Realities," July 1972, Department of Defense.

To sum up, the only people who had a right to ask us to get out of Vietnam after all that had happened were the South Vietnamese, and their behavior shows they did not want us out. That's precisely why I regard the course of action being proposed by my learned opponent as a moral disaster. As to whether the present agreement could have been reached in '69, I don't know anyone in the Communist world who thinks it could have been.

ABRAM CHAYES

I think even the Republicans in the audience will have some questions about the comparison between Abraham Lincoln and General Thieu.

It is true that even in democratic countries there are certain invasions of civil liberties in wartime. It is also true that I don't measure the entitlement to American support purely by the degree to which the recipient lives up to the practices of Western democracies. But the Thieu government is an unusually repressive government. There is no political opposition in South Vietnam. There are thousands of political prisoners. There is no freedom of the press and, indeed, only last week some American correspondents who were seeking to interview the North Vietnamese truce supervision team on its arrival in South Vietnam were threatened with arrest and expulsion from the country.

I do not say that the North is any paragon of democratic virtue. But when Mr. Kaplan argues that the peace has given the South the opportunity to resist totalitarian rule, I think that is Alice in Wonderland terminology.

Mr. Kaplan said a good deal about the success of Vietnamization and the capability of the South Vietnamese forces to defend their country now. I suppose the future will tell about that capability. For myself, I am very dubious. The last performance of the South Vietnamese army was in the spring offensive launched by the North in 1972, not yet a year ago. Everybody, including our own military, agrees that but for the U.S. intervention with massive air and artillery support, the bombing of the North and the mining of Haiphong harbor, the South Vietnamese army would have been overwhelmed, in spite of four years of the brilliant and principled policy of Vietnamization. What is it that makes us think that today, eight months later, and without American support, that army is better capable of defending the South?

Mr. Kaplan objects that the some $14 billion spent in the first six months of 1969 should not be assigned to President Nixon because it was *budgeted* by President Johnson. But I cannot see how it is "arbitrary," as he claims, or even inappropriate to charge President Nixon with responsibility for expenditures made during his term of office, especially since he has claimed unbridled authority, by impoundment or otherwise, not to spend appropriated funds unless he thinks fit.

Finally, let's talk about "bugout." That seems to be a term my colleague, Professor Kaplan, enjoys. The course that I suggest was available to the Nixon administration from the beginning. It's not a bugout. What I am proposing is essentially this administration in 1969 should have sought to reach the kind of settlement that we ultimately did reach in 1973. If it is not a bugout now, why would it have been a bugout then?

There isn't very much new about last month's settlement. It is very similar to the one that was reached in 1954 at the end of the first Indochina War. In fact, it is a good deal less favorable to the South than the 1954 accords; but it is essentially a settlement that recognizes the military realities of the situation on the ground.

The settlement is also not much different from the kind of settlement we reached in 1962 in Laos, where, interestingly enough, we did accept the principle of a tripartite coalition government, one-third right-wing, one-third Communist and one-third neutral. That settlement didn't work, because of the continuation of the Vietnam War next door. But neither was that settlement the prelude to a takeover by the Communist portion of the coalition. And, indeed, in the agreement that we have just reached, we have reconfirmed the 1962 accord on Laos, implicit in which is the tripartite coalition government.

So that one could have expected in 1969 that a settlement recognizing the then military realities, which are essentially the military realities today, could have been negotiated—not in a week, not in a month, perhaps—but in the six or eight months that a skillful diplomat like Dr. Kissinger would have needed to do it.

Mr. Kaplan says, and I agree, that the North Vietnamese demands then being made were "unacceptable." They were unacceptable from Mr. Nixon's standpoint, and that is the perspective I have adopted for this discussion. But it is true that our demands were unacceptable also. Both sides were demanding the fruits of military victory without having achieved that victory.

Now the question that we are asking and must ask, as a responsible power, as citizens of what is still the greatest power in the world, is this: On whom is the onus of making the first move in a situation like that? What is the obligation of a responsible power bearing the burdens and responsibilities that we do in the world? In the Vietnamese situation of the late sixties, was it to impose our will by force, knowing the cost that that entailed, or was it to make a reasonable effort for a compromise settlement?

In my view there is no doubt what the responsible course would have been. I think we are paying the price now for having chosen the other course, and I think we will continue to pay for it in the future.

DISCUSSION

NED BEACH, Senate Republican Policy Committee, staff director: I'm addressing my question to Professor Chayes. You held that we should have followed the course in 1969 which you feel we did follow in 1973. In 1968, then candidate Nixon stated that he had a plan. As a consequence of that plan, I feel there's a difference in the respective strengths of the two antagonists. But most significantly there is another difference that neither debater has mentioned yet and that's the great difference in the attitudes of Russia and China. In my view, both Russia and China have now realized that they have played this war game just about as far as they could, that they have achieved from it all that they could, and that it now is to their benefit to bring it to an end.

When Nixon said he had a plan, he couldn't reveal it. I'm rather certain that this was a fundamentally important part of his plan. I think that was the crucial difference and I wonder if you would comment on that, sir?

PROFESSOR CHAYES: As I welcome the peace, I welcome the rapprochement both with Russia and with China. One of the problems with the Vietnam War and the Nixon war policy was that, far from promoting rapprochement, it posed grave risks to that much more important policy initiative of the Nixon administration. Those risks did not materialize. We are fortunate that they did not. But nobody doubted—not the President himself, not Dr. Kissinger—that many times in the past four years, and particularly last spring when the Haiphong harbor was mined and the bombing resumed against the North, very serious risks were posed to the policy of rapprochement.

Secondly, you suggested that the Russians and Chinese have decided that they've come to the end of their drive for external aggrandizement.

MR. BEACH: Not exactly. What I said was that they had taken as much out of the war as they could.

PROFESSOR CHAYES: Well, I maybe even prefer that formulation. Looking at it from the point of view of the Russians or Chinese vis-à-vis the United States—if you regard that as a basic antagonism—and counting up the respective gains and losses on the two sides, they spent some $4 billion or so on military assistance to the North, while achieving enormous propaganda gains throughout the Communist world, the third world and even in the West. Another consequence of the war, as Mr. Buchan says, is that the authority of the American government is gravely compromised. If you evaluate the matter in terms of competition between the United States and the major Communist powers, the result seems to be a fairly significant set of gains for the Communists.

My own view is that the Russians and Chinese, in some ways like us, are experiencing what one might call a retrocession from a quarter of a century of external activity. They, like us, see that they have many internal problems to deal with, that they may have misconceived the nature of the contest, that the antagonism is not the kind that they first thought it to be, and that the potential gains from this kind of activity are not as great as they had supposed.

My only regret is that we didn't seem to be able to draw that conclusion any sooner than they did.

ROBERT GORALSKI, moderator of the debate: Professor Kaplan, do you want to respond to this question about China and the Soviet Union?

PROFESSOR KAPLAN: I did speak to that point in my opening statement but I guess it went by too fast. I referred to four years of Nixon's diplomacy as providing the Russians and Chinese with incentives for wanting the war settled. Their relationship to Vietnam, their competition in Southeast Asia, the effects in Europe and elsewhere were important too in creating those incentives—so that both of them simultaneously put pressure on the North Vietnamese to come to terms with us.

Now, although at times there were certain embarrassments because of the need to conciliate the North, it is not true that the policy of rapprochement was ever threatened in any serious way by anything that we did, including the mining of Haiphong harbor. What is true is that the Russians were enormously distressed with the North Vietnamese for double-crossing them when Kissinger went to Paris after his Moscow meeting. The Russians thought they had everything set up. Their anger was entirely directed at the North at that point, not at the United States. Nixon's and Kissinger's diplomacy did not run any substantial risks in this respect. Indeed, knowledgeable Eastern European diplomats regarded McGovern's position on Vietnam as irresponsible.

WILLIAM SCHNEIDER, legislative assistant to James Buckley, United States Senate: My question is directed to Professor Chayes. Historically, U.S. foreign wars have been conducted and terminated without significant domestic dissent. In view of the fact that the Vietnam War is widely advertised now as America's longest war, could you describe how the vocal criticism of the Nixon administration's Vietnam policy by opponents like yourself contributed to an early termination of the conflict?

PROFESSOR CHAYES: I think that a democratic country cannot maintain a war policy, a policy of large scale resort to armed force, unless it has the general support of its people. There have always been some dissenters but, as you say, very few of our wars involved a significant split in domestic opinion.

The opposition to this war by opponents of all stripes did demonstrate that there was not united American support for either the objectives or the methods that we were pursuing. The opposition was placed on a variety of grounds, some moral, some prudential, some in terms of the other priorities that the United States has or should have. But in a democracy those sentiments must be taken into account by whatever government is in power, even if the President prefers to listen to the football game.

RICHARD BUTWELL, State University of New York: Professor Kaplan, in your formal remarks, if I understood you correctly, you said in effect that by the time of the Tet offensive in 1968 the war had been, I think I quote you correctly, militarily won. If this is in fact the case, what would have been lost if the kind of proposal had been made by the President in May of 1969 that was made in May of 1972?

PROFESSOR KAPLAN: The war had in effect been won in this sense: The Viet Cong had suffered very serious defeats and the North Vietnamese divisions in the South had been beaten. But the ARVN (South Vietnam's army) no longer resisted as an organized fighting force—although that's not completely true because there were differences among the ARVN divisions then as there are today. However, the war had been won in a projective sense. That is, it had been brought to the point where, with a resolute policy and public support, we could have established an independent South Vietnamese government that was assured of remaining in office. The difficulty was that when Johnson stepped down, the lack of public support for a continued American presence made the maintenance of that position impossible.

Military victory is perhaps an overstatement. I didn't mean that at that point we were where we were on September 2, 1945, with respect to Japan or on May 8, 1945, with respect to Germany. I meant that the end of the war was in sight. You could see the military victory ahead but, as a country, we were not prepared to do those things necessary to consolidate the victory—which meant making sure that the government of South Vietnam had effective police and military forces.

EDWARD O'BRIEN, *St. Louis Globe-Democrat*: A question for Professor Kaplan. In view of everything that has happened in the past four years, what is the future of South Vietnam, of Indochina and, in particular, of the principles for which we believe we were fighting in Indochina?

PROFESSOR KAPLAN: I don't know what principles we thought we were fighting for. The one point where I agree with Professor Chayes is that no administration ever articulated these principles in the way that I think they should have been articulated—particularly Kennedy and Johnson. I was distressed about this and made several trips to Washington to talk about that failure.

But essentially you are asking me the following question: Can I predict the future in South Vietnam? Will there be a non-Communist, surely nontotalitarian, relatively nonauthoritarian government? I think it depends upon a number of factors that I'm not capable of predicting, namely: How intelligent will President Thieu be? Will the inevitable accidents of politics work to his advantage or go against him? Now, one well-known opponent of the war, Professor Popkin at Harvard, has made a $100 bet that President Thieu will be in power in 1976, which at least suggests that it is not a foregone conclusion that he'll be out.

As a political scientist I'm wary of making extensive predictions. In 1948 everyone said that the Greek government was going to collapse in the face of the civil war. In 1954 everyone said that Diem would be out in six months. While Diem's government developed very serious weaknesses later he surely was not out in six months. In 1955 I helped write a book for the Brookings Institution which stated that there would be very serious fissures in the Communist bloc, and everyone who reviewed the first draft of the book said we were crazy—a response that led to institutional modifications.

In short, I'm saying that none of us is an expert on this. I think under the circumstances there is a reasonable probability of survival for a non-Communist South Vietnamese government and that there would not have been this reasonable probability if President Nixon had not held out at least for the present terms. I would have preferred better terms but at least the present terms are adequate.

But to call this a victory one has to ask: a victory in terms of what? Certainly, if you had asked me in 1961 whether it would be worth spending what we've spent since then to achieve the present situation, my answer would have been clearly negative. We've paid a huge price for it. But if you ask me whether it's been worthwhile to keep going since our commitment of late 1963, well—though perhaps not in the stupid way in which we did—I'd have to say yes. This is true also of the situation since 1969. I think the price of getting out in the wrong way would have been more substantial than the price of staying in.

PROFESSOR CHAYES: May I make a short response? I think you have to ask what chance there can be for any government that has presided over a war in which, all told about 2,000,000 people, one in every nine in South Vietnam, were killed or wounded, in which some 8,000,000 or half the population were made into refugees in the whole 12 years of the war, where the economy was shattered, the traditional way of life and social structure pulverized and the land itself disastrously scarred? Let me repeat one of Frances FitzGerald's conclusions: "After 13 years of a major war, South Vietnam has become ungovernable, a mass of refugees, an ecological disaster and a catalog of social and economic ills. Those who rush or are rushed into taking responsibility for this anarchy are bound to be repudiated in the long run."

That's an opponent of the war talking. But General Thieu is a supporter of the war and he doesn't seem to rate the settlement too highly in terms of his own chances for survival

45

either, Mr. O'Brien. In fact, he has been even less enthusiastic about it than the American peaceniks.

KENNETH LANDON, School of International Service, American University: With respect to this quantification of the losses in blood and treasure, I've seen an estimate that it would take about 88 days to replace all of the people who lost their lives. So I'm not overly impressed with the quantification.

But that isn't my question. Professor Chayes, you said that Nixon rejected negotiations in May of 1969. I would like to suggest that what Nixon did in May of 1969 was to submit, as a basis for negotiations, the terms which were eventually accepted in 1973. They were rejected at that time, much to the shock of Scotty Reston who wrote a column about 30 days later asking, Don't the leaders in Hanoi realize that President Nixon has offered them what they wanted?

Theoretically, Nixon had three real options when he came into office. One, he could choose a military solution. He promptly rejected that, which left him with only two. Either he could accept the enemy's terms or he could fall back on the classic ploy of diplomacy: when you don't know what to do, don't do anything in the hope that something will turn up. I thought that the last was going to be his choice until he came out with his proposal of May 1969. That proposal was rejected, as you very properly indicated. But then Nixon made a trip around the world, in July and August, and when he indicated at Guam that geography makes the United States a Pacific power, I think he was creating a new frame of reference for negotiations. The reason I believe this is that the secret negotiations led by Dr. Kissinger began in August at the completion of this round-the-world trip. So it seems to me that, about the time of Guam, Nixon was indeed projecting the negotiations which Kissinger launched in August 1969.

I'd like Mr. Chayes to comment on that.

PROFESSOR CHAYES: A lot of this is going to have to wait for historians, Dr. Landon. But as to the point you address specifically, I think Mr. Kaplan and I agree that in May 1969 President Nixon opted for the policy of Vietnamization—that is, pursuing the war, winding it down, as he said, but pursuing it nonetheless—and not for a policy of negotiations.

Now it's true that, like any head of state who makes such a decision, Nixon did have a political position, a negotiating position. That negotiating position was far from—in fact, it was essentially different from—the one ultimately settled upon. He said our position was, first, complete withdrawal of all non-South Vietnamese forces from the South, and that meant specifically the North Vietnamese. It was, second, that the Thieu government would stay in power, with its ultimate fate to be decided after the withdrawal of the North Vietnamese by supervised elections.

Now he understood, and I think Mr. Kaplan will agree, that in the situation at that time, those demands on our part were just as unacceptable—because they were the political counterpart of military victory—as the North Vietnamese demands were unacceptable to Mr. Nixon. It was not until we abandoned the demand for North Vietnamese withdrawal and the insistence on a political settlement before the end of the war that they responded and we reached the ultimate compromise. My position is that if we had taken that step in the beginning—I don't mean just as propaganda—if we

47

had seriously undertaken the option of negotiation at that time, we would have reached the same result four years earlier.

PROFESSOR LANDON: But haven't you overlooked part of that text in which President Nixon called for the withdrawal of North Vietnamese troops and then he went on to say, But if you allege that you are not there, I won't argue the point?

PROFESSOR CHAYES: No, he didn't go on to say that.

PROFESSOR LANDON: Yes, he did. That's exactly what he did say.

PROFESSOR CHAYES: Not in 1969.

HOWARD PENNIMAN, Georgetown University: I find asking a question very difficult when a number of the statements made seem to me to be of at least marginal accuracy. It is difficult to understand how one can talk about what might have been done in 1969 when as recently as the fall of 1972 one of the candidates for the presidency was still arguing that the best that the United States could do was to achieve simple withdrawal of all troops, the end of the Thieu regime, and the release of prisoners of war at the pleasure of Hanoi—though, of course, we would encourage Hanoi to release them.

But the question that I want to raise is in an area where it seems to me some of the stronger overstatements were made. Professor Chayes suggested that there is really no difference between the South Vietnamese government and the North Vietnamese government. I would submit that if you take almost any standard of what is or is not a popular government that, while one might not give A grades to either of the regimes, one cannot give the same F grade to both.

Let me note that in the competition for the two houses of South Vietnam's legislature in the last election, 1970, 160 candidates ran for 30 Senate seats and the vote was divided in such a manner that the winners had somewhere in the neighborhood of 25 percent of those cast, and 1,200 candidates ran for 159 House seats, about eight for each seat, and again the winners got something like 20 to 25 percent of the votes cast. The contrast with the situation in the North is fascinating. Since 1946, North Vietnam has had four sets of national assembly elections and no incumbent, not one, has been defeated in any of the four. Not only that. In 1971, the last elections, three-fourths of the winners got better than 95 percent of the vote. Contrast this with the situation in the South in which only 40 out of 137 won reelection and of those 40, 21 were members of the opposition.

Now surely one cannot really talk of these two regimes as equally totalitarian.

PROFESSOR CHAYES: I'm not defending the regime in the North. I don't have to defend it. I am saying that the quality of the regime in the South is relevant in determining how much effort and how much expense and how much cost on our part was justified to save it. As far as your statistics on elections are concerned, I'm sure they're accurate, if you cite them. It is also true that once those people got elected to the legislature, it did exactly what President Thieu told it to do.

PROFESSOR PENNIMAN: No, that is simply not a fact.

PROFESSOR CHAYES: Yes, when the issue came to who was going to run against President Thieu and who was going to reverse the Supreme Court view that Ky could run, the

49

legislature reversed. They did exactly what they were told to do.

PROFESSOR PENNIMAN: No, that's just factually wrong. What happened was that Ky decided not to run, just as Minh decided not to run. This was not a reversal of the court's decision. It was not a reversal of the legislature.

GENE LA ROCQUE, Center for Defense Information and United States Navy (retired): I have a question in two parts for Professor Kaplan, and perhaps for Professor Chayes also. First, what specifically, professor, did the United States gain by waiting four years for a settlement in Vietnam? And, second, what specifically did the United States lose by waiting four years?

PROFESSOR KAPLAN: It's essentially the same question and I think the answer to it is relatively simple.

But, first, I want to dissociate myself from words that were put in my mouth by Professor Chayes. I think that Nixon went into the negotiations in 1969 with a dual strategy: one of reaching a negotiated settlement, if the North was willing to reach such a settlement on reasonable terms, and the other of pursuing the policy of Vietnamization, if the North wasn't. The problem arose not because Nixon wasn't willing to reach a compromise settlement in 1969 but because there wasn't a single iota of response in the private talks until after the Russians had brought pressure to bear upon the North Vietnamese prior to the 1972 spring offensive—and then got double-crossed anyway until very late in the game just before our November election.

I think this relates in part to the question that was brought up earlier about the political opposition in the United States.

50

After all, the North Vietnamese had scored an enormous victory in 1968 when they had forced an incumbent U.S. President out. They couldn't be sure that they couldn't do the same thing to Nixon, or at least force him to reach a settlement before the 1972 election that would turn the South over to them on a silver platter. So it's quite understandable that they absolutely refused to negotiate, except on terms that would have meant a bugout by the United States. Of course, one U.S. presidential candidate presented just such a platform and did it quite openly—even speaking of the fact that the president of South Vietnam would flee.

Would there have been consequences had we pursued such a settlement? I was traveling in Asia in September 1972— indeed, at the same time that *Newsweek* was quoting Professor Chayes, whether accurately or inaccurately, as saying in Europe that the United States had no security interest in Asia, or in Japan. In Australia, a Labor party member who is close to Whitlam, the present Prime Minister, said to me despairingly, "Maybe we ought to pull out of ANZUS and appear as remote and inconspicuous as we can." In Malaysia, when I suggested that perhaps the United States was showing some credibility in Vietnam, a man who I'm told is a potential future prime minister responded: "Don't tell me anything like that. You don't have any opportunity to get out."

I think getting out in 1969, without ensuring Northern nonintervention or maintaining important support for the South, would have produced very serious consequences, consequences quite different from those of not having gotten in in the first place. The whole situation in Asia and then in Europe would have come unstuck. And that's not a minor

51

matter. Instead of the period of détente we're moving into now, we would have moved into a very, very difficult situation, both in Asia and in Europe. We were stuck. There's a term I won't use before the cameras about where they had us. In my opinion, the North was playing a very hard and resolute game and until Nixon was able to structure the situation so that it was to the disadvantage of both China and Russia to continue that game, there was no way for us to get out from under, except by surrendering.

ADMIRAL LA ROCQUE: Could I restate my question for you, professor?

PROFESSOR KAPLAN: Surely.

ADMIRAL LA ROCQUE: What did we gain specifically by waiting four years and what did we lose?

PROFESSOR KAPLAN: I told you very specifically what we've gained. We have avoided a situation in which our entire diplomacy and the world political balance would have come unstuck. You may not regard that as a specific gain. Perhaps you regard it as a general gain—in which case I will avoid your question by stating that here is an important general gain.

What have we lost? We've lost money. We've lost men. There has been an additional deterioration in our balance of payments.

PROFESSOR CHAYES: It's fairly easy to say the world would have come unstuck if we hadn't stayed in Vietnam for four years, but that's one of those statements that not many people are going to be able to prove. In fact, it's a little hard for Professor Kaplan to have it both ways: to argue that on the one hand the Russians and the Chinese were so anxious for the détente that they put pressure on the North Vietnamese to come to terms but that, on the other hand, if we had come to terms earlier the diplomatic situation would have reversed itself.

The fact is, I think, that the circumstances moving the Russians and Chinese to détente and to the kinds of accommodations we've come to are very much more profound. They represent very much greater changes in the world than do the activities around that odd-shaped table in Paris.

PROFESSOR KAPLAN: I didn't say that.

PROFESSOR CHAYES: I said, it's hard to link American diplomacy and the policies of China and the Soviet Union.

PROFESSOR KAPLAN: Would you like me to do it specifically? I will.

PROFESSOR CHAYES: Admiral La Rocque asked you to do it specifically twice. [Laughter.]

PROFESSOR KAPLAN: No, he asked me for specific advantages of our policy, not to make the specific linkage.

GEORGE WILL, *National Review*: I would like to ask Professor Kaplan to make the specific linkage and Professor Chayes to dissolve it if he can. It seems to me that the gravamen of your thesis, Professor Kaplan, is that both the Soviet Union and China had strong incentives by mid-1972 to pressure Hanoi to accept a settlement that (a) did not remove Thieu and (b) did not humiliate the United States. The magic word in town these days is linkage, and you are postulating a certain linkage between American diplomacy and this change in Communist policy. Specifically your thesis rests on two axioms—I think necessarily. The first is that our cooperation with China and the Soviet Union is important to these countries in some critical way and, the second, that our cooperation was linked to some credible threat to withdraw the cooperation unless they helped us settle the war.

So I have three questions for the two of you: Have I stated your axioms correctly? What were the benefits involved in the cooperation that we credibly threatened to withdraw from the Soviet Union and China? Once we made that threat credible, what did China and the Soviet Union actually do to end the war?

PROFESSOR KAPLAN: Remember that the Soviet Union began making nuclear threats against China in 1969 and, while it's by no means clear these threats were anything more than bluster—although some people believed them—the Chinese launched an extensive civil defense program, became very worried and started reading Nixon's speeches very carefully. There was one piece in *Foreign Affairs* before the election, and another statement almost immediately after the election. To spell out in detail the considerations that made it impossible for China to respond before the "ping-pong diplomacy" would require an expertise in internal Chinese politics I don't have, although I think the change is related in part to the Lin Piao affair.

The rest of the story from the Chinese standpoint is, of course, that China required some sort of understanding with the United States to counter this sort of Soviet pressure. At the same time the Soviet Union, in its linkages with India and South Vietnam and other countries, was trying to build a *cordon sanitaire* around China so that the Chinese would not be able to withstand a total American withdrawal from Asia.

The Chinese policy shift is explained domestically in China—whether the explanation is serious or not I'm not competent to answer—by the argument that since the United States is a weaker power which will withdraw in the long run anyway, China doesn't have to be worried about the American presence. Peking is more worried by the Russians coming in and filling the vacuum.

For their part, the Russians began to get very worried about the U.S.-China linkage and, as late as December of '71, were paranoid about it. You would hear talk in Moscow about the yellow peril, and the Russians were having dreams of some vast American-Chinese alliance against them. It became very important to the Russians to do something to prevent the American-Chinese détente from going too far.

This was done in a number of ways, SALT being one—although that's a very complicated business which doesn't fit in simply. There were other pressures in the Soviet Union with respect to SALT that crosscut the pressures for détente. In a few minutes I can't go into these. A second way, very important to the Soviet Union, was to demonstrate that despite the American linkage with China there was now a duopoly of world power involving the United States and Russia. In other words, the USSR was a world power on the way up and wanted to stress this linkage. Finally there were certain very important economic reasons for the new Soviet attitude.

So what happened was that from the standpoint of both China and the Soviet Union, the damage being done to the United States in Vietnam was now outweighed by the need to use the United States in other ways. This is the specific linkage that the Nixon diplomacy worked upon. Precisely what would have come unstuck if we had not remained resolute in Vietnam is hard to say. We would not have been a good potential partner to China, for instance. I can't predict what would have happened in China internally, except—you know, perhaps, where Lin Piao's plane was supposed to be flying, and that flight suggests one possibility. But there are a half dozen others I could mention as well.

Sure, I can't be very specific about how this would have come unstuck or how it would have affected the Japanese, because very different futures might emerge from similar beginnings, but the idea that our security interest was not directly involved in Vietnam and that there would not have been a feedback to Europe is one I regard as absurd.

PROFESSOR CHAYES: To get back to a somewhat narrower question than the one Mr. Kaplan has answered. I think it follows from his answer that there were very big currents in world politics starting long before 1969—at least as far back as the missile crisis—and moving in the direction of détente or of some sort of restoration of more normal and less antagonistic relations between the United States and China and the United States and Russia.

Those were very powerful currents in the world situation and I suggest they would have culminated in this rapprochement within a comparable time period, whatever happened in Vietnam. The Vietnamese issues were essentially side issues—they were, to use terminology that Mr. Kaplan may be familiar with, noise in the system. They complicated matters. I've no doubt that he is right that the Russians and the Chinese put pressure on the North Vietnamese to settle. But they never cut off supplies. How much that pressure meant to the settlement in the final analysis, how much the broader movements of world politics meant, is very hard to say. My guess is the interactions were marginal. The rapprochement was going to take place and developments in Vietnam had their own dynamics. The two linked in a marginal way but neither affected the other decisively.

MODERATOR GORALSKI: Thank you very much. Our sincere thanks to our distinguished panelists and our special thanks to Professor Chayes and to Professor Kaplan.

Thank you and good evening. [Applause.]

PART TWO
Two Insiders' Views

LECTURES

G. WARREN NUTTER

The real question before us today is whether we should have surrendered to North Vietnam in 1969 instead of reaching an honorable settlement in 1973. To understand why the question must be put in this way, we must project ourselves back to the time when President Nixon took office.

Our forces were then moving into, not out of, Vietnam. The troop ceiling had risen to 549,500, and the buildup had achieved such momentum that onboard strength did not reach its peak until a month after the President's inauguration.

We had suffered some 31,000 combat deaths, and the weekly rate had soared to 562 only nine months earlier. In January 1969, it was above 300.

Wartime mobilization had been in effect only a matter of months in South Vietnam. Those under arms amounted to fewer than 425,000 regulars and 400,000 others, all poorly equipped, poorly trained, and poorly led. Modern rifles were a rarity for the ground combat troops. South Vietnam's air force contained fewer than 130 combat aircraft. Its navy did not have the capability of engaging in serious combat on the rivers, let alone at sea. All South Vietnamese forces were almost completely dependent on us for logistical support, including maintenance. We had not entrusted them with any significant combat responsibility, and we had no plans for molding them into a force capable of defending their country against the external threat. The most we had done was to begin planning, on a crash basis after Tet, to equip and train South Vietnamese forces to meet the internal Viet Cong threat.

The South Vietnamese economy was in a fragile state, totally dependent on our largesse for such prosperity and stability as it enjoyed. Our financial support was being dispensed in ways that encouraged irresponsibility and waste, since our policy was essentially to guarantee U.S. financing of any budgetary deficit that would generate an inflation of more than 30 percent a year. Consequently, South Vietnamese taxes remained low while governmental spending soared, and the annual gap between imports and exports grew to around $725 million, or some 45 percent of gross national product (GNP). We had done nothing to prepare the way for a stable, self-supporting, and expanding economy, and we had no plans for doing so.

The enemy was known to be holding 328 Americans as prisoners of war. Another 990 Americans were missing in action and unaccounted for. Although bound by the Geneva Convention, the enemy steadfastly refused to honor its solemn obligations. We, on our part, maintained an official policy of silence on the prisoner question, keeping the world ignorant of the plight of our prisoners.

A quarter of the people and half the hamlets of South Vietnam were controlled in some degree by the enemy. The legitimate government had only recently been established as an elected body after years of turmoil and government by coup. The enemy enjoyed sanctuary for its infiltration routes, supply corridors, and staging areas in Laos and Cambodia—

in the latter case with the consent of the then-established government.

Within the international context of that time, the Vietnam War had been made into a confrontation between the United States, on the one side, and the Soviet Union and People's Republic of China, on the other. Consequently, the latter, as Hanoi's patrons, placed their full weight behind the demand for unconditional political victory in the South, and provided material support accordingly. Given the atmosphere of confrontation, neither Moscow nor Peking perceived that it could gain something important from the United States if it modified its stance in Southeast Asia.

Hanoi, although suffering a severe military defeat in the Tet offensive, had scored a great psychological victory in the eyes of the world at large as well as the United States. The climate of dissension here at home encouraged Hanoi to stand fast on its political demands, despite military disaster. North Vietnam knew military victory was beyond its grasp, but it had reason to believe that, sooner or later, public opinion would compel political capitulation by the United States.

Given strong unity on the one side and disunity on the other, Hanoi absolutely refused to negotiate until the legitimate government of South Vietnam was overthrown. Meanwhile, our government had placed all its chips on a threefold policy of maintaining large U.S. ground forces in Vietnam to counter the external threat, preparing the South Vietnamese to cope only with the internal threat, and hoping for a satisfactory settlement at Paris. Such a policy had no place for withdrawal of U.S. forces except through a negotiated settlement. On the contrary, that policy depended on an undiminished U.S. presence as the means for achieving success at Paris.

Though delegations had been assembled in Paris for some nine months, no negotiating worthy of the name had taken place. None was in prospect as long as we refused to impose a Communist-dominated government on South Vietnam or ratify one imposed by conquest. There was no chance of separating a military settlement from a political one.

This, then, was how things stood at the beginning of 1969. What courses of action were open to a new administration? Military victory in the classic sense had to be ruled out because the public would not have supported those measures required to achieve it. For that reason and because there was no prospect of help from Hanoi's patrons, an immediate settlement ensuring self-determination for South Vietnam also had to be ruled out.

Only two possibilities remained. The first was to acquiesce by withdrawing U.S. forces immediately and unilaterally and permitting the legitimate government of South Vietnam to be overthrown—in other words, to bug out. The second was to stand constantly ready to negotiate while turning responsibility for defense of South Vietnam over to its own forces and undertaking creative diplomacy that would give Hanoi's patrons a stake in an honorable settlement.

There is no need to mince words: the first course would have been surrender on whatever terms the enemy might have been generous enough to provide. Under the best of circumstances, it would have taken time for our forces to leave. Six months was sometimes mentioned, but withdrawing 540,000 men in 180 days means withdrawing 3,000 a day, a prodigious task to say the least. There would have been no hope of evacuating the billions of dollars worth of supplies and equipment supporting our forces.

Above all, there would have been grave perils in such a course of action.

First, our troops would have been dangerously vulnerable. No military maneuver is more difficult to execute successfully than a retreat, and there was no assurance that the enemy would not strike at our retreating forces once substantial withdrawal had taken place. On the contrary, the leaders of North Vietnam made no secret of their eagerness to be history's instrument in smiting the giant of the capitalist world.

Second, the only way to get our prisoners back would have been to make our foreign policy hostage to Hanoi. North Vietnam had always reserved the right to demand some mixture of economic and political ransom in exchange for our prisoners. Since we had not even mobilized world opinion on the prisoner question, Hanoi could have extracted an intolerable ransom, political and economic, for the return of our prisoners. The sky could have been the limit.

Third, aggression would have been rewarded. In the times and circumstances, unilateral withdrawal of U.S. forces would have sealed the political doom of South Vietnam and condemned it to domination through aggression.

Fourth, there would have been a vengeful bloodbath. Given the history of terrorism and vengeance in Southeast Asia, no one can doubt that South Vietnam would have been subjected to a systematic and bloody reign of terror.

Fifth, there was the peril of destroying the world's confidence in our fidelity and reliability. We had undertaken a solemn commitment to protect the right of self-determination for the South Vietnamese. In the eyes of the world, that commitment was writ large, with the full weight of legitimate authority behind it, as manifested by a treaty linking us to the Southeast Asia Treaty Organization (SEATO), the Tonkin Gulf Resolution (passed by the Congress, incidentally, 504 to 2), an expeditionary force of more than half a million troops, and continual congressional appropriation of funds to support the war effort. There was not the shadow of a doubt about this commitment. Who would place faith in our reliability if such a commitment, so heavily engaged, had been so lightly repudiated—if those taken under our protection had been so cavalierly abandoned to their own meager defenses? What would have been the consequences for NATO, the keystone of our security? What deterrent force would have remained in our commitments anywhere? What foreign policy could have been built on a reputation for perfidy?

Sixth, there was the peril of irreparable damage to American self-respect. The nation has suffered enough from guilt feelings about loss of life in Vietnam. The suffering would be far more profound and prolonged if we had to live with the sense of shame and self-reproach that would have accompanied a dishonorable settlement of the war. On this score, there is no more eloquent testimony than the patriotic words of gratitude uttered by our prisoners of war on coming home, some after seven to eight years in captivity.

"Honor," says the dictionary, "denotes a fine sense of, and a strict conformity to, what is considered morally right or due." A man of honor keeps his word, and so does a nation of honor. Those who scoff at the importance of honorable relations among nations have the heavy burden of revealing how peace could exist in a world of perfidy, and how the United States could wield constructive influence in world affairs if its honor were under a cloud.

Nor is it more reasonable to argue that, when the going got tough, the time had come to abandon our commitment to South Vietnam. A nation's word means little if it can be taken back when it is most needed, or whenever the nation giving it has second thoughts about whether its own national interests are still directly promoted by the commitment. The ultimate commitment of a nation is to go to war, and we had gone to war after passage of the Tonkin Gulf Resolution in August 1964. The time to weigh the consequences of that act was then, not four years later. Having engaged ourselves so profoundly, we could not honorably abandon our commitment to the self-determination of South Vietnam unless carrying it out would have created catastrophic consequences for our own nation.

The second section of the Tonkin Gulf Resolution, passed almost without dissent by both houses of Congress, left no room for doubt about the depth of our commitment:

The United States regards as vital to its national interest and to world peace the maintenance of international peace and security in southeast Asia. Consonant with the Constitution of the United States and the Charter of the United Nations and in accordance with its obligations under the Southeast Asia Collective Defense Treaty, the United States is, therefore, prepared, as the President determines, to take all necessary steps, including the use of armed force, to assist any member or

protocol state of the Southeast Asia Collective Defense
Treaty requesting assistance in defense of its freedom.

The words are clear and precise. They constitute a more
firm commitment than we have made even to the defense
of NATO.

But the commitment was "to take all necessary steps" to
assist the South Vietnamese, not to fight the war for them.
Up to 1969, we had fought the war for them, and we had
done so in a way that imposed an unnecessarily profound
burden on us without showing promise of defending their
freedom. Fortunately, there was another course open to an
honorable fulfillment of our commitment.

The American public understood what was at stake and
supported that course as it was charted by President Nixon.
It called for active diplomacy and Vietnamization to proceed
together as both complementary and alternative modes of
resolving our participation in the Vietnam War. Our troops
were to be withdrawn in accord with success in negotiation,
the level of hostilities, progress in Vietnamization, and provision for returning our prisoners and accounting for those
missing in action.

Vietnamization had three phases. The first consisted in
turning responsibility for ground combat over to South Vietnamese forces. It was completed by fall 1971. The second
phase, which transpired concurrently with the first but took
longer, consisted in building a self-reliant capability for air,
naval, artillery, logistical, and other support activities. The
third phase, now under way, involves reducing our presence
to a military advisory role or less, depending on progress in
implementing the Nixon Doctrine in that part of the world.

Vietnamization got under way with accelerating speed in 1969 as large numbers of our forces were withdrawn, elaborate and detailed plans were formulated for training and modernizing South Vietnamese forces, and substantial progress was made in carrying out those plans. Some 65,000 U.S. forces came home by mid-December 1969, and some 115,000 by mid-April 1970. At this point, unfortunately, success of the entire program was seriously endangered by the deteriorating situation in Cambodia.

Under the government of Prince Norodom Sihanouk, much of Cambodia had become a staging area and supply zone freely, although not flagrantly, utilized by North Vietnamese and Viet Cong forces. The policy of our government had been to permit those forces to enjoy sanctuary in Cambodian territory, some of it as close to Saigon as Baltimore is to Washington. Sihanoukville had become a primary point of entry for enemy supplies, and enormous stockpiles had been built up over the preceding years in privileged supply areas.

By early 1970, Cambodians had had enough of the encroaching domination of their country by an alien power and use of it to launch warfare against a neighboring state with which they wished to be at peace. Their sentiments were manifested in public demonstrations demanding withdrawal of North Vietnamese forces and in the patriotic surge of support for the government of Lon Nol after the ouster of Sihanouk as chief of state during his March visit to Moscow. Rebuffed in his efforts to negotiate directly with the North Vietnamese and to reactivate the International Control Commission within Cambodia, Lon Nol issued a call for military assistance from friendly powers to help his weak forces prevent the imminent takeover of his country by North Vietnam.

Such a takeover would have removed the last elements of restraint on flagrant North Vietnamese military operations along the entire western flank of South Vietnam, from Sihanoukville through Cambodia and Laos to the borders of North Vietnam. The security of our withdrawing forces and the success of Vietnamization would have been imperiled.

Under the circumstances and in response to a Cambodian plea for help, President Nixon took the only course of action open to him. At the end of April, some 20,000 U.S. and South Vietnamese troops were sent into Cambodia to destroy and disrupt sanctuaries. The success of this incursion is a matter of history. Denial of sanctuary was, in itself, a decisive element in the future course of Vietnamization. At least equally important was the damage to the enemy's supplies and supply routes, particularly the closing of Sihanoukville (renamed Kompong Son) to enemy traffic.

Success in Cambodia and progress in Vietnamization permitted us to withdraw our forces at an impressive rate. Our troop ceiling was reduced by some 140,000 in 1970, 160,000 in 1971, and 167,000 in 1972. By fall 1971, as already noted, we had withdrawn all ground combat troops except a small contingent required to provide security for other remaining forces, and the South Vietnamese had assumed full responsibility for fighting on the ground. In four years, the troop ceiling was cut from 549,500 to 27,000, or by an average of more than 130,000 a year. Under the terms of the cease-fire agreement, virtually all remaining U.S. forces are to be withdrawn by the end of March 1973, as our prisoners come home.

Our casualties fell apace. Combat deaths ran around 9,400 in 1969, 4,200 in 1970, 1,400 in 1971, and 300 in 1972. Any men killed in action are too many, but at least the number fell to about the same level for the entire year 1972 as for a single week at the beginning of 1969.

Meanwhile, South Vietnam became stronger in almost every relevant respect. Its armed forces increased by almost a third, rising from 824,000 to 1.1 million. In addition, paramilitary forces rose from 1.3 million to 4 million. Within the armed forces, the navy and marine corps doubled in size, and the air force multiplied two and a half times. More than half a million members of the armed forces received basic and specialized training in Vietnam each year. Some 10,000 were sent abroad for training in advanced skills, many of them to the United States. The latter included pilots, mechanics, navigators, engineers, intelligence analysts, and key commanders and staff. The enormity of the task of training such highly skilled personnel is reflected in the fact that, before they could undertake technical training, they had to master a foreign language, predominantly English.

Vast quantities of equipment were supplied over the last four years to these trained and tested men: over 942,000 small arms and crew-served weapons, 1,600 artillery pieces, 51,000 radios, 61,000 wheeled vehicles, 2,800 tracked vehicles, 1,800 fixed and rotary wing aircraft, and 990 naval craft. In addition, some 600,000 less-modern small arms, such as carbines, were provided to paramilitary forces.

As rapidly as they were being trained and equipped, the South Vietnamese were gaining experience and confidence through having combat responsibility thrust upon them. The

71

ultimate test came with the invasion of 1972, when, after three years of preparation, North Vietnam brought the full weight of its military power to bear on the defending South Vietnamese forces, including an attack by four divisions with massed artillery and armored forces across the narrow front of the Demilitarized Zone (DMZ). Those who would belittle the courageous defense by the South Vietnamese would do well to remember that they took on the burden of ground fighting that Americans had borne in the Tet offensive four years earlier. Moreover, they confronted a more powerful conventional offensive by main forces. The North Vietnamese were soundly defeated. In the end they managed to hold only a small fraction of territory (not containing a single provincial capital) and a much tinier fraction of the population.

The economy has shown similar progress, having taken long strides toward self-generating stability and growth. After careful study, the Nixon administration inaugurated a policy of linking U.S. economic assistance to introduction of responsible fiscal practices and creation of a favorable climate for initiative and enterprise in South Vietnam. The South Vietnamese government responded on its part by introducing a set of important economic reforms beginning in fall 1970. The various fiscal and financial reforms then and later were successful in cutting the rate of inflation in half during 1971, creating a flexible foreign-exchange rate, and establishing an institutional framework conducive to long-run stability and self-sustaining growth. Although the gap between imports and exports remains large, it has fallen by more than $100 million (in current prices) since 1969, or from some 45 percent of GNP to some 27 percent. Despite the shock of the North Vietnamese invasion, exports almost doubled in 1972, and inflation amounted to only 22 percent as compared with 32 percent in 1969.

The significance of economic progress has been nowhere more evident than in the ability of the South Vietnamese economy to absorb the shock of the 1972 invasion. By then, the economy had ceased to be one of the weakest links in Vietnamization. The newly found resilience of the economy was sufficient to enable the government of South Vietnam to enact additional tax reforms in fall 1972, in the midst of heavy fighting, that have paved the way for long-range fiscal stability. The South Vietnamese economy has a long way to go before it can stand on its own feet, but it would be difficult to find an example of an underdeveloped economy under such stress in time of war that has managed to go as far as this one in addressing problems of long-run stability and growth.

Politically, the authority of the legitimate government spread in width and depth as Vietnamization proceeded, bringing with it a sense of personal security that enabled schools to run, commerce to function, and the ordinary business of life to proceed outside a realm of paralyzing fear. The contrast of before and after was nowhere more striking than in the Delta, a Viet Cong stronghold in the throes of constant conflict during the late sixties, but a thriving agricultural community governed from Saigon by 1972. The North Vietnamese invasion set pacification back in the immediately threatened areas, but by January 1973 less than a tenth of the people were controlled in some degree by the enemy, as contrasted with a quarter in January 1969.

Concurrently with Vietnamization, we were busily engaged on the diplomatic front. In May 1969, Hanoi reaffirmed its position in the form of ten points, which restated the demand that the United States unconditionally withdraw its forces and remove the Thieu government before any other matters could be discussed. Supported by Saigon, President Nixon countered with a proposal that the two sides negotiate on the following combination of items: staged mutual withdrawals, internationally supervised elections, and early release of prisoners of war. In an effort to break the deadlock, Henry Kissinger initiated private talks with the North Vietnamese in August 1969, and met secretly with them thirteen times during the next two and a half years.

All efforts to negotiate were fruitless. In September 1970, the other side reformulated their position into eight points instead of ten. The modification was insubstantial, amounting to a statement that they would discuss release of our prisoners and safeguards for our withdrawing troops provided we first set unconditionally a deadline for unilateral withdrawal of our forces before July 1971.

A month later, in October 1970, President Nixon offered, with the backing of Saigon, a completely new proposal consisting of five points: an Indochina-wide cease-fire, a multi-nation peace conference, a negotiated withdrawal of U.S. forces, a search for a political solution, and immediate release of prisoners of war. Although these are virtually the same terms that were agreed to in January 1973, Hanoi absolutely refused to discuss them in 1970. It is important to note that our side made an important concession in not calling for mutual troop withdrawals. We were intentionally silent on the question of North Vietnamese withdrawal in the hope that such a concession would remove a sticking point in negotiations. The other side was made fully aware of our flexibility on this matter. For example, on June 15, 1971, Secretary Rogers denied in a press conference that we were calling for mutual withdrawal. Throughout this period, we repeatedly stated our willingness to negotiate on every issue but one: the right of self-determination for South Vietnam.

The other side seemed to bend a little in summer 1971, when a seven-point proposal was issued by spokesmen for the Viet Cong Provisional Revolutionary Government. It appeared that there might be some shift on the prisoner question: the other side now said it would agree to modalities for release of prisoners provided we first set unconditionally a date within 1971 for total withdrawal of our forces. Previously they had offered only to discuss the question. Grasping at straws, we intensified our secret talks only to discover that nothing had changed but rhetoric.

We made one more major public effort in January 1972, proposing elaborate provisions to ensure a fair election in South Vietnam. The other side rejected the proposal on the ground that it did not provide for dismantling of the legitimate government. Their ultimate response to our negotiating efforts of more than three years was to launch a massive invasion across the demilitarized zone on March 30, 1972, in flagrant violation of all accords and understandings.

Fortunately, we had been diplomatically active elsewhere as well. From the very beginning of his administration, President Nixon had stressed his goal of moving from confrontation to negotiation, particularly in relations among superpowers. We became engaged in discussions with the Soviet Union on a broad range of issues, from strategic arms limitation to trade. We opened contacts with the People's Republic of China, culminating in the President's visit to Peking in February 1972. From these diplomatic initiatives, bilateral mutual interests emerged within the triangular context that came to transcend conflicting interests in Vietnam. Both the Soviet Union and the People's Republic of China, each for different reasons, acquired a stake in an honorable settlement of our participation in the Vietnam War. It was therefore no surprise that President Nixon's visit to Moscow went ahead on schedule in May 1972, only two weeks after our mining of Haiphong harbor.

Suffering from a military defeat, confronting dwindling support from their patrons, and facing a presidential election in the United States with a certain outcome, the North Vietnamese finally agreed in October to negotiate a settlement by offering to separate military and political issues. On January 27, 1973, they signed an agreement on virtually the same terms that we had proposed more than two years earlier.

Nobody wanted to take four years to reach that settlement, but nobody came forth with a feasible shortcut. I spent those four years as assistant secretary of defense for international security affairs, and I was not made aware of any shortcut that would have avoided the perils sketched above. Perhaps my worthy predecessor, whom I have the honor of debating tonight, knew one. If so, he did not publicize it, nor did he leave it behind in the files after his year and a half in the same job.

Aside from the loud cries of a few to bug out, most responsible criticisms of our efforts in 1969 amounted to quibbles about the pace of Vietnamization or to schemes for tacit negotiation through mutual example. Averell Harriman and Cyrus Vance, who had suffered ample frustration in their efforts to negotiate explicitly with North Vietnam, advanced several proposals in the latter category. Signal our good intentions to Hanoi, they said, by pulling out troops or reducing the intensity of combat or declaring a cease-fire in place or doing something along these lines. Then watch and see how Hanoi responds, in the hope that it too will take some constructive action to signal its good intentions. Throughout, Harriman and Vance were proposing ways to hasten genuine negotiations leading to an honorable settlement. In the face of the failure of our many concrete signals to elicit any constructive response from North Vietnam, one has good reason to doubt that Harriman and Vance offered anything more likely to succeed. In any event, to the best of my knowledge, neither advocated in 1969 that we abandon our commitment to protect South Vietnam's right of self-determination.

Clark Clifford's article in the July 1969 issue of *Foreign Affairs* created something of a stir, being viewed at the time as one of the bolder critiques of existing policy. When read today, it assumes a blander tone and becomes recognized as merely a variant of Vietnamization. In that article, Clifford clearly endorses the basic concept of Vietnamization in every relevant respect. He proposes withdrawal of 100,000 U.S. forces by the end of 1969; in fact, 115,500 were withdrawn by spring 1970. He goes on to advocate publication in advance of a promise to withdraw all of our ground combat

77

troops by the end of 1970, or nine months earlier than the date at which responsibility for ground combat was in fact turned over to the South Vietnamese. Here we come to a fundamental difference in judgment: Clifford argued that the South Vietnamese could successfully assume the responsibility for ground combat within 18 months; President Nixon disagreed. I find little in the history of Vietnamization to support Clifford's prediction, since we proceeded with Vietnamization at flank speed. The Clifford article, incidentally, suggests no timetable for withdrawal of the bulk of U.S. forces and reaffirms our commitment to protect South Vietnam's right of self-determination and to prevent a bloodbath.

Beginning in late 1969 and early 1970, criticism of Vietnamization took on a sharper tone, and attention became focused on demands that we set a deadline (usually 18 months from whenever the proposal was made) for withdrawal of all U.S. forces. For example, in May 1970 Clark Clifford switched from the position taken in his 1969 article and advocated the setting of such a deadline. There were many variations on the common theme, some implying abandonment of our commitment to South Vietnam and others not. Most proponents of such a deadline specified that adherence to it should be contingent on getting our prisoners back within a definite period. But, during the presidential campaign, the Democratic candidate explicitly argued for unconditional withdrawal of our forces, rejecting any linkage with return of our prisoners. I submit that none of these proposals offered promise of moving us toward an honorable settlement. Indeed, on the very eve of such a settlement, a candidate for the highest elective office in the land was advocating a bugout that would have left our prisoners at the mercy of the enemy. It is not clear what effect that spectacle had on Hanoi's leaders at such a late point, but it can hardly have made them more eager to reach a settlement.

And so, as we look back, four years passed before we achieved an honorable settlement. The simple fact is that what needed to be done could not be done in less time. Over a million South Vietnamese had to be trained and equipped as armed forces to safeguard the American withdrawal while assuming full responsibility for defense of their country. They assumed that responsibility as it was thrust upon them so successfully that more than nine-tenths of the people now live under the protection of the legitimate government. The way had to be prepared for South Vietnam to stand on its own feet economically and politically. The world had to be made aware of the plight of our prisoners. Something had to be done about the sanctuaries in Laos and Cambodia. The American people had to be brought together again. Our stance as the world's policeman had to be supplanted by the Nixon Doctrine. And the context of international relations had to be restructured, as it was so dramatically through President Nixon's historic visits to Peking and Moscow, so that the polarized confrontation of superpowers could be replaced with a more promising diplomacy of peace that cast the struggle in Vietnam into proper perspective for all.

That is why the Vietnam settlement had to come in 1973, not 1969. Those four years have brought our prisoners home without ransom. They have caused aggression to go unrewarded. They have permitted us to fulfill our commitment: South Vietnam now has the opportunity to take care of itself, to determine its own future, and to thwart a bloodbath. The same four years have made reconcilation with North Vietnam a realistic prospect and preserved a stabilizing role for us in Southeast Asia.

The world retains confidence in our fidelity and reliability. And Americans have preserved their self-esteem.

PAUL C. WARNKE

There are those who contend that the Vietnam settlement is not a proper issue for debate. Why, they argue, should any question now be raised? What purpose can it serve? Is not all criticism pointless or worse? Is it not just sour grapes?

Some administration spokesmen have strongly maintained that there must indeed be no debate—that all Americans should unite instead in acclaiming this settlement as the earliest possible and the only possible way to gain peace with honor.

I am glad that the American Enterprise Institute does not agree and that it has scheduled this series of three debates on the Vietnam settlement. The institute, as I see it, is right in its view that such key foreign policy issues as this should be subjected to the test of rational debate—even in the euphoria of a cease-fire, at least for American forces, and in the joy of freedom for American prisoners. Pride in their courage does not automatically rub off on the cause with which we burdened them.

Vietnam has been the overshadowing issue of American foreign policy for ten years. How we got there and why we stayed so long at such cost demands reasoned analysis. And the answers to these questions bear directly on the issue of whether the settlement reached in late January of 1973 is significantly better for American interests than the kind of settlement that might have been reached four or five years earlier.

Many Americans urged in 1969 and thereafter that we negotiate to get ourselves out of Vietnam and to get our prisoners back. No one can prove that a settlement then would have been substantially identical with the one finally reached in 1973. I shall not try to do so. Almost certainly it would have been quite different in supplementary detail. But the real issue is not when this particular agreement could have been achieved, but rather whether American interests would have been satisfied by the kind of resolution that might have been achieved in 1969 or even earlier.

It is important, I repeat, to debate this question for at least three reasons:

First, by overvaluing the details of the present settlement we can find ourselves reinvolved militarily in Southeast Asia. In my view, the present settlement is a good one simply because it does provide for the withdrawal of our remaining forces and for the return of American prisoners of war. This is enough. It is all that realistically we should have hoped for after years of disillusionment. With our military presence removed, the political future of Vietnam can be and should be left to the Vietnamese. But if we undertake the job of policing the cease-fire and preserving the framework of the settlement of January 1973, we assume again the uncongenial and futile task of trying to solve foreign political problems with American military force. We should, of course, support the multi-national structure established in the hope that differences can be peacefully resolved. But its possible failure should neither surprise us greatly nor drive us into an active role in a third Indochinese war.

A second reason for debating whether we should have negotiated our way out of Vietnam in 1969 or before is to help us understand better the continuing nature of American security interests. If we can do that, we can hope to avoid ever again becoming embroiled in an inordinately expensive and divisive conflict extrinsic to these basic national concerns. For if we leave Vietnam under the impression that our national security was advanced by our involvement there, and by the details of this settlement, then we are more apt to make the same mistake again, for the same ill-considered reasons. We will have learned nothing about the distinctions between those things we may not like and those which involve our vital interests. In our relief we should not confuse surcease with success. Because it feels so good to stop this war, there is some risk that we may begin to believe it was worth starting. Our security interests will be best served if we consider carefully whether we got into Vietnam much too readily and stayed much too long.

A third reason for this debate is that public dialogue about important and controversial issues of policy is basic to a democratic society. I do not think we can afford the anomaly of presidential monopoly in national security affairs. At a time when international factors intrude deeply on every aspect of our domestic life, the field of foreign policy must be subjected to more intensive and more informed scrutiny. This will not guarantee us against future mistakes. It will, however, ensure that tough decisions are the product of true democratic processes. At a minimum, this should dampen later recriminations and bring about the broad consensus that is needed in order for any foreign policy to be effective.

Of course involvement in Vietnam was not the result of a decision by one President or by one party. For a couple of decades a succession of Presidents and Congresses participated in the process of getting us involved there. And they had the help of the national security bureaucracies, broad academic approval and the editorial agreement of most American journalists who claimed foreign policy expertise. Throughout the Kennedy and Johnson administrations, Richard Nixon, in his role as a major Republican spokesman, applauded our Vietnam effort. On February 15, 1962, he expressed the hope that President Kennedy would "step up the buildup." In a speech on April 18, 1964, he called for pursuing the enemy into Laos and North Vietnam. By August of 1966, he was advocating that U.S. forces in Vietnam be increased to 500,000 men.

This popular support, though impressive in magnitude, was shallow in analytical content. Our leaders, most of us assumed, must know what they were doing. Democracy demands, however, more informed participation than this. The nature and timing of our disengagement from this unhappy adventure should receive broader thought than attended its initiation. We should all help to see that the right lessons are learned.

As a small contribution to this debate, I wish to support the thesis that a settlement could have been and should have been reached in 1969 and indeed earlier. It is not a partisan position. I think there is plenty of blame to go around. As I see it, there is not and never was any security interest that justified our going to war in Southeast Asia. The shifting rationalizations that have been employed to justify American military participation confirm my view. None has withstood the test of time. Our role there was never necessary to prevent worldwide conquest by international communism. It was never needed or even feasible as a means for containing China. The struggle there was not a test case for Communist "wars of liberation." And our interest in freedom and self-determination for the South Vietnamese should have been no different than it was for the Biafrans, the East Pakistanis or the Namibians of Southwest Africa. We wish freedom for the world, but we should know now that American bombs do not spread freedom. They only destroy the native soil in which it can take root. Our firepower can protect us from attack. It cannot save alien societies from themselves.

It seems to me significant that, both at the outset and at the conclusion, our concern about Vietnam and our interference there with the process of indigenous if troubled development rested largely on considerations outside Southeast Asia itself. The results should lead us to question whether in fact we have had an Asian policy or whether, instead, we have treated local Asian problems as primarily an element in global relations with our West European allies and our Communist rivals. Implicitly, we seem to have proceeded on the outmoded colonialist assumption that Asians can have no serious problems of their own, but only those that derive from the concerns and the conflicts of the Western world.

The indications are that President Franklin Roosevelt was prepared, after World War II, to resist French reoccupation of Indochina and to encourage the nationalist movement headed by Ho Chi Minh. But our engrossing foreign policy concern at that time was the restoration of morale in Western Europe in order to help resist the spread there of Soviet influence. Any further blow to French prestige from the loss of its Indochina colonies was deemed too damaging for a French government faced with a strong internal Communist threat. So we threw our weight against Vietnamese nationalism.

The success of the containment policy directed against Soviet expansion in Europe also contributed largely to our blunder in Vietnam. The threat to Western Europe—and hence to us, because of our major interest in keeping the human and industrial potential of Western Europe out of hostile hands—was a combination of overt military aggression and of internal Communist parties that seemed to owe allegiance to Moscow. This threat was met by providing the centuries-old and developed countries of Western Europe with restored military and economic strength bolstered by a formidable American military presence.

The trauma of China's "loss" to a Communist takeover and the prospect of a partnership in hostility between the Soviet Union and the People's Republic of China led to quite understandable apprehensions in the late 1940s and 1950s. In Asia, as earlier in Europe, we feared a drive to bring a major part of the world into a Communist monolith.

In particular, the defeat of Chiang Kai-shek by the Chinese Communists and Peking's prompt recognition of Ho Chi Minh drastically altered the American perspective on a civil war which had already been raging in Vietnam for four years. In our minds it became pivotal to the containment of Red

China. In a speech to a conference of newspaper editors about the time of Dien Bien Phu's final agony, April 1954, Vice President Nixon advocated the dispatch of American troops if needed to stave off French defeat. Years later, in the fall of 1967, Secretary of State Rusk sought to justify our Vietnam involvement by pointing to the prospect of "a billion Chinese armed with nuclear weapons." And Mr. Nixon, campaigning in New Hampshire in February of 1968, described Vietnam as "the cork in the bottle of Chinese expansion in Asia."

The analogy to our European experience has proven not only inapposite but disastrous. A China bent on physical conquest on the Asian mainland could not have been contained by treating the emerging and incompletely realized small countries of Indochina as if they were Western democracies with a strongly developed sense of nationality and with the combined potential to resist major military attack. But the futility of a containment policy in Asia was offset by the fact that no containment was necessary. China has directed itself instead, with varying degrees of success, to dealing with its own massive internal problems. The reassertion of its claim to Tibet and its response to the presence of American forces in North Korea near its boundaries did not presage a continuing campaign to expand its control by military means.

In fact, the threat of overt Chinese aggression was never clearly delineated as the principal reason for our military intervention in Vietnam. Instead, we based our concern in the 1950s and early 1960s on the "domino theory." The danger, according to this doctrine, was that if South Vietnam fell into Communist hands, this would lead to Communist governments in Laos, in Cambodia, in Thailand and ultimately elsewhere in Asia. Whether the dominoes would tumble before a Chinese shove or whether they would collapse from internally generated pressures was never specified. The risk of their fall was thought in itself to be a sufficient threat to American security. So motivated, we accepted the guardianship from which the French were forced at Dien Bien Phu.

By the early 1960s, Chinese Communist rhetoric about "wars of liberation" as the wave of the future provided a somewhat more plausible rationale for our continued and increasing participation in the Vietnamese civil war. Overt aggression was, we told ourselves, not the gravest threat in an era in which the shadow of nuclear strategic weapons inhibited major military action by the superpowers. Instead, we concluded that techniques of counterinsurgency would be essential to our own survival and success. The ferment of emergent nationalism in the erstwhile colonies of Asia thus became equated with recurrent past efforts of one or more European powers to dominate their neighbors and thus the world.

As the decade went on, more and more doubt was cast upon this thesis. It became apparent that we had grossly overestimated the ability of our military might to overcome both the conviction of the North Vietnamese leaders that the southern half of what they regarded as their country must be freed from foreign domination and the resistance in the South to continued control by a Western-sponsored regime. Nor, by the late 1960s, was there any new support for the supposition that Chinese-inspired insurgency would spread throughout

Asia. We found ourselves in the increasingly unpopular and untenable position of fighting a native people to win their acceptance of a governmental apparatus of foreign creation.

As the Nixon years progressed and we relaxed our attitude toward China, our continued military action in Vietnam was again rationalized in terms of our global interests. We were cautioned that an American "loss" through unilateral disengagement would lessen the prestige of the American President and make it impossible for him to negotiate effectively with other great powers. But "balance of power" explanations are as inadequate as those based on some fancied strategic value in Indochinese real estate. The key questions—why we should replace the French in resisting the reunification of Vietnam under the strongest political party, why we should do so at the cost of hundreds of billions of dollars, of more than 50,000 American lives and of festering divisions within American society, why we persisted in sustaining a parody of Western democracy in Saigon at the price of centuries of Vietnamese culture and a generation of Vietnamese youth— are questions for which no valid explanation has been given. No valid explanation exists.

We have failed until now to look at Vietnam realistically in terms of its own problems and prospects. Too apocalyptic a world view has blurred our perception of smaller and local events. We thus concluded that we must stop communism in Indochina even if this meant saving an alien people from the consequences of their own decision. But history should have taught us that military strength is of utility only when used to meet military aggression. It has never served to fight ideas. Ideological competition cannot be resolved finally on the battlefield.

In the years since 1969, the war has expanded geographically even as our physical presence diminished. Cambodia has been pushed from its neutral tightrope and four-fifths of its territory is now controlled by forces friendly to Hanoi. Souvanna Phouma's influence in Laos has eroded under Communist pressure and American bombs. Self-determination for South Vietnam has become a code word for continued one-man rule by President Thieu which offers little more freedom than the Communist dictatorship in the North.

For those who reject the above analysis, for those who believe that vital American interests were in fact at stake in Vietnam, that the other Asian countries were lined up as teetering dominoes and that fighting in Vietnam was the way to prevent World War III, then our involvement in Vietnam was necessary and wise. But for them even the 1973 agreement should seem foolish and risky—because it leaves South Vietnam's fate in doubt and its very sovereignty ambiguous. If survival of an independent non-Communist South Vietnam is vital to our security, we were right to get involved and it is the 1973 settlement that is wrong.

I do not believe this, nor do I think many others would be willing to make such an assertion. I agree instead with Dr. Kissinger's recent statement that the Vietnam conflict is and was a civil war. I do not think the result there was ever crucial to the interests and the interrelationships of the great powers. Most of us, I believe, had reached these conclusions by 1969. And once it became clear that Vietnam did not engage any important American security interests, then our overriding objective in negotiations should have been the speedy and safe withdrawal of all American forces and all

89

American prisoners. An agreement based on this objective, in my view, could have been achieved years before now.

The solution would not have been an ideal one. But ideals have never fared very well in this war. The bitter divisions in Indochina would have continued. Four more years of war have done nothing to heal them. For an indefinite time, continued fighting might have left thousands dead and other thousands homeless. The same bleak record has been run up since the Paris settlement in January. Then, as now, removal of our military presence would have left the contending indigenous parties to sort things out among themselves. Promises of no reprisals would have been as easy to obtain, and no harder to enforce. Our true international security interests would not have been damaged by earlier acceptance of the fact that they were never engaged in Vietnam.

Our negotiating goals forever exceeded our interests. We let ourselves become embroiled in a game where each side piled demand on demand in order to avoid showing weakness. The United States government did not propose in 1969 or 1970 or 1971 the safe withdrawal of American forces in exchange for the safe return of American prisoners of war. In his television interview with Messrs. John Chancellor of NBC, Eric Sevareid of CBS and Howard K. Smith of ABC on July 5, 1970, President Nixon emphasized his insistence on mutual withdrawal as a requirement in any negotiated settlement: "We are prepared by negotiation to bring out all of our forces and have no forces at all in South Vietnam if the enemy will negotiate, if they will withdraw theirs." On April 17, 1971, in an appearance before the American Society of Newspaper Editors, he observed that "we will have a total withdrawal in 12 months if they would be willing to mutually withdraw their forces." It was not until January 26, 1972 that Dr. Kissinger informed a press conference: "On May 31st, we proposed a withdrawal of American forces. We were prepared to set a deadline for the withdrawal of American forces and the exchange of prisoners. This was the first time that the United States had indicated that it was prepared to do so unilaterally; that is to say, without an equivalent assurance of withdrawal from the other side."

But the proposal made public at the beginning of 1972 was not the simple offer of withdrawal of our troops in exchange for our prisoners. It was conditioned on North Vietnam's acceptance of a winner-take-all presidential election in South Vietnam within six months, with President Thieu remaining in complete power until his ceremonial withdrawal and replacement by a Saigon proxy one month before election day. And despite the absence of "equivalent assurance of withdrawal from the other side," the proposed settlement would have imposed unacceptable restrictions on the presence of North Vietnamese troops in the South. Even one-for-one replacement was proscribed by the requirement that "there will be no further infiltration of outside forces into any of the countries of Indochina." The principle of mutual withdrawal continued in President Nixon's peace proposal of January 25, 1972: "Among the problems that will be settled is the implementation of the principle that all armed forces of the countries of Indochina must remain within their national frontiers." The agreement offered would have embodied the concept of two Vietnams, with the DMZ as a national boundary, not the mere military demarcation line set forth in the 1954 Geneva accords. It called for capitulation by the other side, not compromise.

When we had hundreds of thousands of men in Vietnam, we had the bargaining leverage for a solution based on withdrawal of American military forces and repatriation of American prisoners. It would then have been in the obvious interest of the North Vietnamese to accept such a proposal. And repeatedly they hinted at such interest. For example, Ha Van Lau, then North Vietnam's second-ranking negotiator in Paris, stated on December 18, 1969: "If the United States declares the total and unconditional withdrawal from South Vietnam of its troops and those of the other foreign countries in the U.S. camp within a six-month period, the parties will discuss the timetable of the withdrawal of these troops and the question of insuring the safety for such troop withdrawal." Thereafter, he indicated, talks about a provisional coalition government would be held by the Vietnamese. In June of 1971, members of the Hanoi negotiating team told both California Representative Robert Leggett and *Washington Post* correspondent Chalmers Roberts that the military issues of U.S. withdrawal and the release of prisoners could be settled if the United States would set a date and even though the Thieu regime remained in power in Saigon.

North Vietnam's main negotiating objective has always been the elimination of the American military presence. In that objective, I submit, the real interests of the United States and North Vietnam have always coincided, and the basis for settlement between the two countries has always been present. In the final analysis, it was not bombing that brought Hanoi around but our willingness to get out and to leave the North

Vietnamese army in the South and the Viet Cong in control of its own turf. This is the essence of the agreement from their standpoint.

From our standpoint, what we have sought to gain other than safe withdrawal and safe return of American prisoners is less clear. The uncertainty is compounded by the events that occurred between Dr. Kissinger's October announcement that peace was at hand and the eventual agreement three months later. North Vietnam was ready in October to sign the agreement that Dr. Kissinger described. It was we who demurred and insisted on perfecting changes. The Christmas bombing of Hanoi, and our own heavy losses to North Vietnamese air defenses, seem thus to have served to overcome lingering resistance in Saigon and in Washington, not in Hanoi. We signed in January essentially the agreement for which the North Vietnamese had been pressing in October.

Some differences do exist between the October and January versions, but they seem to me almost frivolous: some ambiguous rhetoric about the DMZ, some changes in the description of the function of the National Council on National Reconciliation and Concord and a modest increase in the size of the supervisory forces are the most apparent. For this, we paid a disproportionate price—in money, in human misery and in world prestige. We gave the world an example it did not need of the use of force to make a political point. Many Americans were led to question whether their own political system genuinely works so as to give the people, through Congress, any control over their fate. Those who would authorize or approve such drastic action to obtain minor textual revisions have a far different view than I do of American national interests.

The agreement reached in January 1973 may be marginally better than that which was feasible in 1969. It may, however, be worse. A settlement then could have left Cambodia with an accepted government in stable control of all but the eastern fringes of the country and all but a fraction of its people.

In Laos, unkindly but accurately described as "a notion, not a nation," the political situation may not have been much better than it is today. It could hardly have been much worse. And its tragic inhabitants would have been spared four years of a rain of death unmatched in bombing history.

We had more troops to bargain with in 1969 and far fewer American prisoners to bargain for. We would have been out of the way then and the Vietnamese would have been compelled to settle their own differences. Instead, 20,000 more American lives were lost and other tens of thousands of Americans were wounded, maimed or permanently disabled. We spent an additional $50 billion and helped bring about our present balance-of-payments and monetary crises. In return we won the privilege of continued entanglement in the murky politics of Southeast Asia.

Rather than the clear solution of simple withdrawal, we find ourselves with responsibilities to a multi-national supervisory force and to the preservation of a cease-fire. The cease-fire will be truly effective only at such times as both Hanoi and Saigon believe that the political current is moving in their direction. And a breach of the cease-fire will present the risk of a new American military involvement. The Vietnamese civil war is not over, nor is it clear enough that we are finally out of it.

The tragedy of Vietnam was that peace for us was always at hand—but for too long, and in both Democratic and Republican administrations, we lacked the will and the wisdom to grasp it.

REBUTTALS

G. WARREN NUTTER

Mr. Warnke has focused primarily on the question of why we should not have gotten into Vietnam in the first place, rather than why it should have taken us so long to get out. I don't intend to debate that question this evening. I do not believe that it would be fruitful to debate why Vietnam. The question tonight is why 1973.

It is suggested that there were opportunities in 1968 and 1967 to reach a settlement, and that again is not the question. The question is: what about 1969 as opposed to 1973?

There were important differences. I will not repeat the situation that existed in 1969, but I do want to consider what could have been done in the way of negotiation, given the international climate at that time.

Mr. Warnke has said, in effect, that there is not a nickel's worth of difference between what we achieved in 1973 and what we could have gotten four or five years ago. He says 20,000 men have been killed during those years and that this is a cost far beyond what we have gained. As a factual question, let me correct the figure immediately—it is not 20,000, but 15,000. I will not quibble, however, except to point out that more than three-fifths of the 15,000 were killed in 1969. Combat deaths that year were 9,400—and over 8,000 of them occurred in the first nine months. These losses reflected the momentum of battle that persisted at that time by virtue of policies followed in the past.

It is not a question of partisan issues. Rather, it is a question of the facts at that time.

Now, what was the negotiating situation in 1969? Here I think we need to be sure that we aren't indulging in fairy tales, because the history is plain. It is utterly false to claim that there was any way in which the United States could have reached an agreement in 1969.

It is sometimes suggested that we could have done so if we'd only compromised on a simple political issue. But the question was not one of compromise. The sticking point was a persistent refusal on the part of the North Vietnamese to negotiate. They refused to negotiate. One has to negotiate before one can compromise. Instead, the North Vietnamese, then and almost four years thereafter, merely issued a series of demands that they said must be met unconditionally by the United States before they would even talk about negotiating. So there was no negotiating possible. There was no compromise possible. It was inconceivable that the United States could have reached an agreement in 1969, in 1970, in 1971, or even 1972 on anything approaching the terms that we have achieved at this point.

It has been said that the present administration insisted on mutual troop withdrawals for more than three years. That, too, is not correct. The initial proposal in May of 1969 was for mutual staged troop withdrawals. In October of 1970, however, the President proposed withdrawal in exchange for prisoners and a cease-fire, without insisting on mutual withdrawal.

So I will close by saying that there was simply no possibility of reaching an agreement in 1969 because there was no possibility of negotiation.

PAUL C. WARNKE

Obviously there is no way of proving a negative. All I can say is that we didn't try. We didn't try in 1968, we didn't try in 1969, we didn't try in 1970, we didn't try in 1971, we didn't try in 1972. During all of those years both sides played the game of "can-you-top-this" negotiations. Neither side had the courage or, I think, the wisdom to come through with any sort of acceptable proposition.

As far as the issue of mutual withdrawal is concerned, I would suggest to Dr. Nutter that as late as June of 1971 the White House, in correcting a previous statement that it thought might be misinterpreted, said that President Nixon was still insisting on mutual withdrawal, that withdrawal of American troops from South Vietnam would be conditioned on the withdrawal of North Vietnamese troops from South Vietnam. That appears to have been the break issue. More than the bombing, more than anything else, it was movement on this issue that eventually brought about the possibility of a negotiated settlement.

As I've said, no one can prove that we could have had a settlement in 1968 or thereafter. I thought we could have had one at that point. I still believe that we could have. I believe that a settlement at that time would in effect have left the political fate of Vietnam to the Vietnamese. That's where it's left today. That's where it belongs.

99

The important issue is to see to it that we leave it there and that American firepower does not again cut across the grain of indigenous development in Southeast Asia.

Thank you.

DISCUSSION

WILLIAM ANDERSON, *Chicago Tribune:* A question for Mr. Warnke. Many people believe that the diplomacy of the Nixon administration with Russia and especially with China had a great influence on bringing about the settlement of the war at this particular time. We did not have the kinds of relations with China in 1969 that we have today. What is your view of this?

MR. WARNKE: It's very difficult, Mr. Anderson, for anybody to assess the relative weight of different factors in this kind of equation. I have no doubt that the attitudes of China and the Soviet Union had some bearing on the situation. But I recall that back in 1968 the Soviet Union was quite anxious to help bring about a resolution of the conflict. I have no doubt that it was in 1969 as well. I had the feeling then that, since the Soviet Union was the principal financial supporter of the North, we could have utilized its influence to a greater extent than we did at that point.

I think that one of the interesting areas of speculation is what might have been done in 1968 and 1969—to pick a bipartisan period—in enlisting the support of the Russians and the Chinese. What I'm saying is that we didn't really try and that consequently we don't know. Now no one can say whether we would have ended up with a better resolution or a slightly worse resolution then than we have now, but the effort should have been made and was not made. By

1968 and certainly by 1969, it was obvious that our main interest in Vietnam was to get out of Vietnam and we should have tried at that point to exercise innovative diplomacy. Instead, we waited too long.

PROFESSOR NUTTER: Let me add a brief comment. In the course of trying to prepare myself for what I knew was going to be a very challenging contest this evening with Paul Warnke, I refreshed my memory as to what people said in 1969. In the course of doing so, I looked back at some of the statements that Averell Harriman made in that period. Readers and writers of the *New York Times* may recall a long interview in August 1969 in which Mr. Harriman explicitly pointed out that he did not expect the Russians to take any initiative whatsoever with Hanoi but that, if we got an agreement, they might help us to get it implemented. He went on to point out that he considered it highly unlikely that we could establish global linkages through which the Russians would help us to disentangle ourselves from Vietnam in exchange for concessions elsewhere.

Over three years later Mr. Harriman wrote an article that appeared in the *New York Times* on February 12, 1973. In that article he says: "As a result of President Nixon's and Mr. Kissinger's skillful diplomacy, China as well as the Soviet Union are both strongly against the continuation of the war."

WILLIAM BEECHER, *New York Times:* My question is directed to both debaters. Mr. Warnke, as I recall, suggests that the decisive point in breaking the negotiating log jam was the decision by the Nixon administration to drop its insistence on mutual troop withdrawal. Mr. Nutter, as I understand it, argues instead that the decisive point came when Hanoi agreed to separate the military cease-fire from the political settlement.

I wonder if each of you would try to justify your quite different assessments?

MR. WARNKE: There is no way of saying what might have been without engaging in crystal-ball gazing. It seems to me, and it seemed to me in 1968 when I was still with the government, that the real hangup was our insistence on mutual troop withdrawal, that the North Vietnamese saw the war in a very different light than we did. As a consequence, whereas we felt that they were an alien presence in South Vietnam, the North Vietnamese regarded Vietnam as a single country. So I feel that our recognition, tacit though it was, of the oneness of Vietnam was the principal motivating force in bringing about an agreement. I could be wrong; I would be surprised if I were.

PROFESSOR NUTTER: I agree with Paul that it's very difficult to predict what might have been, and I hope that his prediction of what might have been is better than his recent prediction of what was to be. On "Meet the Press" on October 15 of last year, 1972, he was asked: "... what is your appraisal of the [private peace] talks at this stage?" His answer, was: "I think that the chances are very dim of securing a political settlement before the election or within any reasonable time thereafter ... because ... our position still requires the maintenance in power of the Thieu regime." That was the position many people held for a long time, and yet now we have a resolution that does maintain the Thieu regime in power.

Instead of defending my position, I want to stress the evidence presented in my formal statement on the question of mutual troop withdrawal. I focus your attention on President Nixon's proposal of October 1970. You will recall the five points of that proposal:

1. an Indochina-wide cease-fire,
2. a multi-nation peace conference,
3. a negotiated U.S. withdrawal,
4. a search—I repeat, a search—for a political solution, and
5. immediate prisoner release.

Now I ask you what conditions those five points resemble, and I suggest they are very close to the conditions that were reached just recently, on January 27, 1973. There was no requirement whatsoever in those conditions for mutual troop withdrawal.

MR. WARNKE: That was one of the instances in which the White House subsequently amplified the President's statement and stated expressly that mutual troop withdrawal *was* still a prerequisite for any settlement in Vietnam.

RICHARD THORNTON, Institute of Sino-Soviet Studies, George Washington University: It seems to me that one of the important questions we should be considering this evening, one that is directly related to peace in '69 or '73, is the extent of North Vietnam's capability to wage sustained offensive action and, in particular, how it was supported in that capability. Would either one of you gentlemen wish to address himself to that question?

PROFESSOR NUTTER: I'm not sure of the relevance of the question to the topic. Do you mean North Vietnam's capability of sustaining military action now or before—

MR. THORNTON: Now and in 1969. Are the capabilities the same?

PROFESSOR NUTTER: All right. Let me say first that these are not the right years to pick. The year 1969 was just after 1968, just after Tet, and North Vietnam's capability in '69 itself was of course affected by the damage of Tet. It took Hanoi about three years to build up the capability for the massive invasion of '72. By then, its capability was quite strong.

At the moment it is again weak because of the serious defeat that it suffered in the '72 invasion. But it would have the capability, if the past were repeated, of once again building up that strength.

MR. THORNTON: This is precisely the issue. The North Vietnamese do not manufacture their own weaponry; it all comes from outside. Why was it that supplies were cut off in 1973 but were not in 1969? Isn't that the avenue along which we ought to be traveling in this discussion?

MR. WARNKE: I'd like to make two comments on that. First of all, the supply was not cut off. Secondly, it is now irrelevant because, in my opinion, North Vietnam is going to be perfectly prepared to wage the battle now on the political level. That's what they've been looking for for some time. They now have that opportunity.

I would suspect that we ought to be more alert to breaches of the cease-fire by Saigon than by Hanoi. Hanoi's interest is going to be to keep us out; it is going to be very interested in seeing to it that our withdrawal is permanent and that, as a consequence, it can deal with this on a sort of subsurface level with no main force action.

105

PROFESSOR NUTTER: I'm sorry, I can't let that pass unchallenged. It simply is not true that the North Vietnamese have always been prepared to wage the battle on the political front. It's completely—

MR. WARNKE: I didn't say that. I said they are now.

PROFESSOR NUTTER: I thought you said, as they always have been.

MR. WARNKE: No, I didn't.

PROFESSOR NUTTER: All right, I misunderstood you then, and I withdraw the comment.

LESLIE GELB, Brookings Institution: A question for Mr. Nutter. Do you believe that the mining of the harbors in North Vietnam and the bombings of December were major contributing factors toward the peace settlement and, if so, why didn't President Nixon take those actions much sooner?

PROFESSOR NUTTER: The answer to your first question is yes. The answer to the second question is that he was hopeful they would not be necessary because negotiations were under way. The North Vietnamese had indicated that they were seriously interested in reaching a settlement. The settlement was almost reached and then—I'm sorry—I have to back away. You're talking about actions in May and not about the second bombing?

MR. GELB: I'm talking about both. Why didn't he take those actions in 1969 and 1970?

PROFESSOR NUTTER: Why not in 1969? They weren't taken then because there were great fears that both the Soviet Union and the People's Republic of China would react in a hostile way, because of our posture toward those two countries at that time. In 1973 our posture was different.

GARY HOGGARD, American University: My question is directed to Mr. Nutter. You and the President have referred to the 1973 settlement as an honorable one. I wonder if you could specify for us the criteria by which one determines when a settlement is honorable?

PROFESSOR NUTTER: Yes. An honorable settlement is one that accords with the commitments that you have made. The commitment that we had made to South Vietnam is the one that I outlined in my paper, the commitment to preserve its right of self-determination. That commitment was made by this country as heavily as any that I am aware of in our history. Therefore, the only honorable conclusion to the conflict is one in which we do the right thing by living up to our commitment.

ANTHONY LAKE, Carnegie Endowment for International Peace: I have a question on a point of fact. You amended the figure on American casualties from 1969 through 1972 to 15,000. Yet 20,000 has been the figure that's been commonly accepted in magazines, newspapers and elsewhere for many months now. I wondered if you could say how it has been recalculated or how you arrived at the 15,000?

PROFESSOR NUTTER: Yes. These are the official figures from the comptroller's office of the Department of Defense. I have a full table that can be displayed to show these figures. The totals were: 30,614 for the years 1961 through 1968, and 15,315 for 1969 through 1972. For the first nine months of 1969, 8,250. For the year 1969, 9,414. For all of 1972, the last year, 300—a number of combat deaths for that whole year, incidentally, that is about equal to one week's losses at the beginning of 1969.

Table 1
U.S. COMBAT DEATHS—VIETNAM WAR

	Period	Cumulative
1969 Quarter I	3,184	3,184
II	3,156	6,340
III	1,910	8,250
IV	1,164	9,414
1970 Quarter I	1,178	10,592
II	1,698	12,290
III	870	13,150
IV	475	13,635
1971	1,380	15,015
1972	300	15,315
Summary		
1961-68	30,614	
1969-72	15,315	45,929

Source: Office of the Comptroller, United States Department of Defense.

MR. WARNKE: I think that the difference perhaps is between those who are listed as killed due to hostile action and those just plain killed. They're all just as dead and the total exceeds 20,000 in the period '69 through '72.

PROFESSOR NUTTER: My figures refer to those killed in action.

ROBERT GORALSKI, moderator of the debate: And the total of 20,000 included noncombat casualties as well.

CHARLES CORDDRY, *Baltimore Sun:* I have a question for Mr. Warnke. The position you have taken tonight and the position Professor Chayes took last night seems to be that we did not get a settlement in 1969 comparable to the one we got in 1973 almost solely because we didn't try. In taking such a position, don't you have a very heavy burden to say why you think the government of the United States could have gotten an agreement but persisted in not getting one, persisted in continuing an unpopular war? So would you list the reasons why you think the administration continued the war when it wasn't necessary to do so?

MR. WARNKE: I think, Mr. Corddry, that the difficulty was a basic misreading of American security interests. You see, Vietnam was never regarded as important for itself and really not very important in terms of Asia. We got into Vietnam to prevent a rebuke to the French at a time when we regarded them as particularly susceptible to internal Communist upheavals. We got into it because of security considerations in Europe.

Then, having become involved in Vietnam, we invented a lot of reasons for it—invented them not consciously but unconsciously. It was sort of like the Ted Husing lateral. Remember Mr. Husing, who was a colorful sports announcer but didn't really understand football? Sometimes he'd identify the wrong ball carrier and then, when somebody would call it to his attention, there'd be an invisible lateral over to the guy who was actually carrying the ball. Now that tidied up the record but it didn't really reveal much about what was happening on the field.

Vietnam was sort of like that. When one excuse became obsolete we invented another.

Now I suspect that during the past four years the principal excuse for Vietnam has been great power confrontation—not Vietnam for itself but rather the notion that if we didn't get some sort of face-saving solution there, the Russians would pick on us in Berlin and the Chinese would not be receptive.

At one point, the President even suggested, in effect, that if we were simply to withdraw from Vietnam, he might not get an honor guard when he showed up on a state visit.

So I don't think that we really ever looked at Vietnam in terms of what was important there, in Southeast Asia, for American interests. As a consequence, we waited until the point at which we found ourselves in 1973. What I'm suggesting is that the price we paid for these extrinsic considerations was totally disproportionate to any gain we received and that the net minus in terms of world prestige was far more than any plus. Persistence in folly, once folly has revealed itself, is a singularly ineffective means of saving face.

PROFESSOR NUTTER: If I may comment briefly, it seems to me that those who were aware of the alleged failure of this administration to negotiate in good faith—and that, in effect, is the point being made—had a very serious responsibility to speak out and tell the administration to negotiate in this or that way. I have searched the record for 1969 and I do not find any advice of this sort coming from anyone.

There was the already noted proposal of Clark Clifford in July 1969 that was considered to be very radical. Take a look at it again. What he proposed was that we withdraw 100,000 men by the end of 1969. In fact, we withdrew over 65,000 by that time and a total of 115,500 by the spring of the next year. Hardly anything to quibble about. He suggested we reduce the level of hostilities on the ground by reducing pressure on the enemy. This was implicit in our withdrawal. He said we should continue full logistic and air support of the South Vietnamese. And he said we should sit back and hope for reciprocity on the part of the North, while preserving the right of self-determination for the South and avoiding a bloodbath.

One comment he made in that proposal was the following: "There has, in my view, long been considerable evidence that Hanoi fears the possibility that those whom they characterize as 'puppet forces' may, with continued but gradually reduced American support, prove able to stand off the Communist forces."

Clark Clifford advocated Vietnamization.

MR. WARNKE: First of all I'd like to point out that Mr. Clifford is a very independent man. He doesn't necessarily follow all the advice I proffer to him. Second, had that proposal been adopted in 1969, had it been announced in 1969, it could have had a very profound effect on a political resolution to the conflict in Vietnam. What he proposed then was that we withdraw 100,000 men by the end of 1969 and all ground combat troops by the end of 1970.

PROFESSOR NUTTER: No, he did not.

MR. WARNKE: I think he advanced it then.

PROFESSOR NUTTER: No, he did not say that in that article. I challenge you to produce the statement.

MR. WARNKE: I think, Dr. Nutter, that if you look again you'll see that he proposed withdrawal of all ground combat troops by the end of 1970.[1]

---

[1] Note by Mr. Warnke: Clark Clifford, "A Viet Nam Reappraisal," *Foreign Affairs,* July 1969, p. 169: "A first step would be to inform the South Vietnamese Government that we will withdraw about 100,000 men before the end of this year. We should also make it clear that this is not an isolated action, but the beginning of a process under which all U.S. ground combat forces will have been withdrawn from Viet Nam by the end of 1970."

PROFESSOR NUTTER: No, sir, I challenge that. He did not make that statement until a year later.[2]

MR. WARNKE: Fortunately the record is clear, and I think that I have read the article with perhaps a great deal more attention than you.

PROFESSOR NUTTER: Reread it, sir.

MR. WARNKE: I don't have to.

MODERATOR GORALSKI: I think all of us will have to read it to settle this question. [Laughter.]

JOHN McCAIN, United States Navy (retired): First, I'd like to say that I have a great deal of admiration and respect for what's been said by both Dr. Nutter and Mr. Warnke.

The basic question at issue seems to be not the resolution of peace after the war was started but whether we should have been there in the first place. You have suggested, Mr. Warnke, that we should not. I take exception to that view on these grounds: Communism is moving worldwide in three areas—political, economic and military. If the United States fails in its obligations and in its respect for people who are on our side, ultimately we will go down to defeat. This may sound like an oversimplification. It is not a highly intellectual statement, but it is plain, ordinary, straight to the point fact. I've heard many times that we shouldn't have been in Viet-

---

[2] Note by Professor Nutter: On the matter of the proposed withdrawal of U.S. ground combat troops, Mr. Warnke is right in this exchange and I am wrong. I mistook Mr. Warnke's remarks as referring to the proposal to withdraw *all* U.S. troops by a fixed deadline, a proposal not made publicly by Clark Clifford, to the best of my knowledge, until spring 1970 (see *Life,* May 22, 1970). Ground combat troops were, of course, only a fraction of all U.S. troops.

nam in the first place. I say to you that, if the Southeast Asian peninsula were to fall to the Communists, it would create problems inside the United States in the years to come of an order that we might not be able to solve. It would affect trade, as well as the interests of the United States as far as these countries are concerned.

MR. WARNKE: I have, of course, the greatest respect for Admiral McCain. I am sorry to find myself in flat disagreement with his statement. I don't think that what happens to the 17 million people of South Vietnam, largely by their own choosing, is going to have any effect on the balance of power worldwide or on our ability to survive as a free and democratic nation.

ADMIRAL McCAIN: I would like to say that I personally am not in a position to throw 17 million people overboard, but let's not get into that.

MR. WARNKE: I regard it as suicide rather than homicide, sir.

ADMIRAL McCAIN: The domino theory, which intellectuals doubt is relevant to what's going on in the world and has gone on in the world, is a hard fact of life. You can rest assured that if one geographic area falls within the realm of the Communists' power, they will move on to the next one.

MR. WARNKE: I respect that point of view, Admiral McCain, but if it is correct, then the 1973 settlement is an act of insane folly on our part.

LAWRENCE STERN, *Washington Post:* Mr. Nutter, President Thieu expressed himself rather forcefully about two terms of the settlement—namely, the 150,000 or 300,000 North Vietnamese troops left in the South and the establishment of what he called a disguised coalition government in Saigon. Do you feel that he misread the settlement rather disastrously?

PROFESSOR NUTTER: I believe you are referring to the reactions after Dr. Kissinger's return from Paris in October.

MR. STERN: After Paris, yes.

PROFESSOR NUTTER: At that time there was a certain confusion. I am not aware of all the details since I was not in Henry Kissinger's immediate group, but there was confusion between the English language text of the agreement and the Vietnamese text. Each said something a little different. It was as if the other side was trying to get back with one hand what it was giving with the other. The word used in the Vietnamese text for the Council of National Reconciliation and Concord happened to be the same as the word for coalition government. So Thieu had a predictable response.

Now, as to the troops, I'm very sympathetic to the problems that South Vietnam faces, but I find it difficult to see how writing into a piece of paper the requirement that there be no North Vietnamese troops in the South really solves that problem. At one time or another we have tried everything within our power—within the constraints of this war—to prevent those soldiers from being in the South, but without success. I find it difficult to see how having it on paper will do any good.

What was put on paper and what was signed was a provision that there be no replacements, no further troops moving into the South that are not those of the South Vietnamese government. Whatever troops there are in the South cannot indefinitely maintain themselves, if they're not replaced.

But that, I think, is a technical point. Ultimately the question of whether the North Vietnamese troops can be kept out of the South is a question that has been faced these many years.

MR. STERN: My question, sir, was whether you think President Thieu's opposition, which was expressed quite openly, resulted from his having misread the essential terms of the agreement?

PROFESSOR NUTTER: The answer is that the Vietnamese and English texts were different in October, and therefore it wasn't necessary for him to misread. The Vietnamese text was not a faithful reproduction of the English or vice versa.

MR. WARNKE: If I might comment on that, I think that the changes in the texts from October to January are almost imperceptible. As I understand the published reports, they really amount to three: There is some ambiguous rhetoric about the Demilitarized Zone, but it is still made very clear that this is a military demarcation line and not a national boundary. There are some changes, as Dr. Nutter has suggested, in the description of the function of the National Council of National Reconciliation and Concord. I think the principal change there was the dropping of the phrase "an administrative structure"—which presumably, translated into Vietnamese, sounds somewhat governmental.

But as I understood President Thieu's objections to the agreement, they were more basic than that. They had to do with the very existence of the National Council of National

115

Reconciliation and Concord and in particular with its tripartite composition, with the fact that it included neutralists as well as Viet Cong.

Now Dr. Nutter has referred to the fact that in October of 1972 I stated my view that there would have to be a substantial change in the American position before peace could be reached. I still believe that. I think that substantial change took place. But why it took place is something that I can't understand because I think it's almost impossible to find a significant difference between the October text and the January text. And, for these minor textual revisions, we paid an enormous price in terms of world revulsion, of the loss of a substantial fraction of our B-52 force, of 95 to 100 men missing in action and, of course, of the devastation in North Vietnam.

Now, it seems to me an overvaluation of minor details to pay such a price. In my view, the basic substance of the agreement was not changed from October until January; nor was it substantially changed from that which could have been achieved in January of 1969.

PROFESSOR NUTTER: Unfortunately, we don't have the two texts before us, but I will flatly say that that's not correct. There is a substantial difference in the two texts.

As to the statement you made in October 1972, Paul, what you said was that you did not believe there could be a *settlement* as long as we insisted that the Thieu regime remain in power. The Thieu regime is in power. There is a settlement. Your reference was to a settlement, not to peace.

MR. WARNKE: I believe what I said was that a settlement was impossible if we insisted that the Thieu regime be left in total unchallenged control of South Vietnam. It has not been left in that position.

PETER FENN, Westinghouse Center for Advanced Studies and Analysis: My question is for Dr. Nutter. You have made a very good argument for the thesis that we achieved our objectives in Vietnam. You have said that we have achieved self-determination for the South, fulfilled the containment objective and have even been a rather effective world policeman in this endeavor. If this is so, why the response from China? Why the response from the Soviet Union? And, above all, why the celebration in the North at the agreements?

PROFESSOR NUTTER: First of all, let me make a correction. I did not say that we have achieved self-determination for South Vietnam. If I seemed to say so, let me correct that immediately. The statement in my formal presentation was that we have given the South Vietnamese the opportunity for self-determination. We have given them everything that anybody can give them except the will to achieve self-determination. Whether they have that will or not remains to be seen.

We have trained them. We have provided them with sufficient stability. We have provided them with equipment. We have gotten an agreement that says they can sit down at the table with the other party and work out the conditions under which there will be elections, that there must be unanimity, and so on. Therefore, we have given them the opportunity for self-determination. Now, whether we've actually given them self-determination, I cannot say.

117

I would not say that we have functioned in this context as an effective world policeman. Rather, we have been very effective in turning over the job of defending South Vietnam to the South Vietnamese—in getting away from serving as the world's policeman.

Now, as to why China, the Soviet Union, and North Vietnam proclaimed this as a victory for themselves, I certainly wouldn't have expected anything different. What is a little surprising is that *we* have not proclaimed it as a victory.

JOHN KOLE, *Milwaukee Journal:* Mr. Warnke, with your strong feelings, did you have any misgivings about accepting a job at the Pentagon in September of 1966 when the escalation of the war was well along? Did you ever consider resigning in protest during that period? Second, is there evidence that Mr. Humphrey, if elected in 1968, would have accomplished a speedier withdrawal?

MR. WARNKE: Let me deal with your questions in two parts. First of all, I had no misgivings about going into the Department of Defense in September of 1966 because I had explained to Mr. McNamara my distinct reservations about the war. I was very fortunate in serving three secretaries of defense, all of whom were dedicated to winding down the war and extricating the United States from that involvement. As a consequence, I never had any occasion to consider resignation.

Mr. McNamara, during the entire period of time that I worked with him, was doing his best to bring about negotiations, to scale down American involvement, to stop the bombing. Mr. Clifford spent the first 29 days of his year as secretary of defense bringing about a bombing cutback to the 19th parallel; he spent the rest of that year trying to bring about peaceful negotiations. Mr. Laird, during the very brief period of time that I served him, worked very hard for American withdrawal. So there was no occasion for me to consider resignation at any time.

As to what Mr. Humphrey would have done, all I can say is that he has indicated that, if he had been elected President, he would have named Clark Clifford as secretary of state and Cyrus Vance as secretary of defense. I don't think the war could have survived the three of them. [Laughter.]

RICHARD HOLBROOKE, *Foreign Policy* magazine: I think, Mr. Nutter, that you owe it to us to say a little bit more clearly what specifically is the difference between the October and the January agreements. Mr. Warnke says there is none; you simply say he's wrong without backing that up.

PROFESSOR NUTTER: It's very difficult for me to be more specific without having the two texts right here in front of me.

MR. HOLBROOKE: Surely you can point out from memory one or two items that might be different.

PROFESSOR NUTTER: As far as I know, the consideration in regard to the replacement of troops is one. There are people here who perhaps can illuminate the differences. Dennis?

DENNIS DOOLIN, deputy assistant secretary for East Asia & Pacific affairs, Department of Defense: One item that was a distinct and fundamental addition in January was the statement that the International Commission on Control and Supervision would operate with respect for the sovereignty of South Vietnam. How that can be swallowed in the North as a victory I don't know.

MR. WARNKE: I didn't get the last part of your statement, sir.

MR. DOOLIN: I said that the January text requires the ICCS to respect the principle of a sovereign South Vietnam and I wondered how Hanoi could view this as a victory.

MR. WARNKE: All 1,160 of the ICCS's members?

MR. DOOLIN: That's correct, and the 12 nations and the secretary general that are to meet in Paris next month.

MR. HOLBROOKE: But surely you're not maintaining that the purpose of the 12 days of bombing was solely to increase the supervisory commission by some 800 people—

PROFESSOR NUTTER: Let's clear that up. The bombing had nothing to do with differences in texts. The fact is that negotiation had ceased. We were almost at an agreement and then the North Vietnamese ceased negotiating. What was necessary was to get them back to negotiating.

MR. HOLBROOKE: You did say there were meaningful differences between the two texts.

PROFESSOR NUTTER: Yes, there were differences. After the bombing and other actions took place, there were stronger provisions in the final document than there were in the original one.

LYMAN LEMNITZER, United States Army (retired): One of the major differences between the October 26 agreement and the settlement that was finally reached was in the size and the character of the neutral nation supervisory commission. In the October draft North Vietnam insisted on limiting the neutral nation supervisory commission to a total force of approximately 250. In my judgment, as one who had responsibility for the enforcement of the armistice in Korea, this was nonsense. It was a clear indication that Hanoi didn't want a workable and reliable neutral nation supervisory commission and it was one of the major reasons, from my own point of view, these terms could not be accepted.

MR. WARNKE: If I might comment on that, the difference was that they proposed 250 and we proposed 4,000.

GENERAL LEMNITZER: That's right.

MR. WARNKE: We split the difference, so the total ended up as something in excess of 1,000. General Lemnitzer, with 530,000 American men there, we had difficulty keeping the situation in order.

GENERAL LEMNITZER: But that was different.

MR. WARNKE: I find the difference between 1,160 and 250 to be absolutely insubstantial.

GENERAL LEMNITZER: This is the supervisory commission, not a combat force, and there's a great difference in their functions. The duty of a supervisory commission is to report violations. That's all its duty is. It can't stop combat. It can only report.

MR. WARNKE: I would suspect, sir, that it would take many times 1,160 to do even a decent reporting job.

GENERAL LEMNITZER: The 250 number was nonsense.

MR. WARNKE: I regard them both as insignificant.

MR. LAKE: Mr. Nutter, you said that the purpose of the bombing was to make the North Vietnamese negotiate again, not to force changes in the actual text. Why not, then, simply have accepted the October text as it was at a time when the

121

North Vietnamese had stated repeatedly that they favored it? Weren't some of the North Vietnamese problems in the November negotiating sessions the consequence of shifts in the American position as well?

PROFESSOR NUTTER: Yes, that is correct. But I didn't say that the purpose of the bombing was this or that. I said that the *reason* the bombing took place was that negotiation had ceased. There had been negotiations going on. We had gone back and said, There are certain things in this text that have to be changed. Thereupon they began playing around and saying, Well, then this has to be changed and that has to be changed. Then they simply ceased negotiating.

MR. LAKE: Then could I ask what the purpose of the Christmas holiday bombing was?

PROFESSOR NUTTER: Its purpose was to resume the kind of pressure that we had used in the past to try to bring about a settlement of the war.

MR. GELB: This goes back to the question I asked before, Mr. Nutter. You said that President Nixon could not mine the harbors of North Vietnam and launch full-scale bombing before 1972 because of possible Chinese and Soviet reactions. I recollect, I believe, that in 1967 and 1968 you were criticizing President Johnson for not taking those actions. Do you now believe it would have been irresponsible for him to have done so, given possible Chinese and Soviet reaction?

PROFESSOR NUTTER: I was criticizing President Johnson? I don't know of any case in which I made statements on this issue—

MR. GELB: Do you believe Mr. Johnson should have ordered such mining and bombing in 1968?

PROFESSOR NUTTER: I was not in the government or otherwise sufficiently aware of all the problems to make a judgment on that matter.

MR. WARNKE: If I might take Dr. Nutter off the hook, it was not Dr. Nutter. It was Mr. Nixon who recommended mining Haiphong and bombing Hanoi and Haiphong in 1967 and 1968.

HOWARD PENNIMAN, Georgetown University: I find it somewhat strange that we are talking as if the idea of a coalition government, which was proposed by the NLF [National Liberation Front] from at least 1965 onward, has been embodied in the agreements which were finally reached.

As I remember the facts, the NLF proposed that, first, the Thieu regime should be forced out of power and, second, there should be a tripartite coalition composed of a government to replace Thieu, which would be approved by the NLF, a neutral force selected and approved by the NLF, and then the NLF. In other words, the NLF was to be all three.

Now, then, the *form* of the National Council for National Reconciliation and Concord specified in the cease-fire agreement is tripartite, as the NLF and the DRV [Democratic Republic of Vietnam] demanded. But its *substance* is bipartite. This is so because the council's membership is to be made up of people representing the Thieu regime, people representing the NLF, and people who are agreed upon by *both*— which is going to mean that half of the membership will be selected by the Thieu regime and half by the NLF. So we really have a council of two parts, not three—and each has a veto. Compare this with the NLF proposal for a coalition government made up of only the NLF.

123

I would ask each of the speakers to comment.

PROFESSOR NUTTER: Well, I agree. [Laughter.]

MR. WARNKE: May I say I agree too. We did not accept the North Vietnamese proposal whole hog. It was a compromise settlement. I applaud it. I am all in favor of it.

PROFESSOR NUTTER: But I think it's an important—

MR. PENNIMAN: But it is a compromise nonetheless in which the substance is that demanded by Thieu, not that demanded by the NLF.

MR. WARNKE: That remains to be seen, sir.

GEORGE WILL, *National Review:* I am intrigued by Mr. Warnke's praise of Mr. Clifford for having limited the bombing, or advocated limiting the bombing, in an attempt to achieve what you, sir, described as fruitful negotiations. Such negotiations did not happen after the bombing was limited, or after we subsequently ended the bombing, or after we included the Viet Cong at the table, or after we began unilateral withdrawal—all of which were said to be surefire ways of getting fruitful negotiations. And everything we achieved, once we did get negotiations, you now dismiss as trivial, as camouflage, as window dressing. What should we have been negotiating about, if not the things which you now dismiss as trivial?

MR. WARNKE: I think basically what we have achieved is getting our troops out of Vietnam and getting our prisoners back. I think that that was negotiable in 1968, and I think it was negotiable at any point thereafter. But we never made that simple proposal. Had we made it, I believe that the political fallout would have been almost indistinguishable from that which will occur at the present time.

As far as the delay in getting fruitful negotiations going is concerned, my feeling in 1968 was that we were placing far too much emphasis on President Thieu's ability to veto our working out our own interests. I believe we continued to do this during Mr. Nixon's first term. Perhaps the one result of the bombing over the Christmas holidays in 1972 was that, after that, President Thieu couldn't ask for much more. We had walked the last mile with him and as a consequence we could settle.

MR. WILL: If I could just raise one detail on this. It is said that on about October 8 the North Vietnamese agreed to separate the political and military settlements and that, as a result, President Thieu remains in power. Is that a trivial achievement in your judgment?

MR. WARNKE: I am sure it's not trivial for President Thieu. But it is almost nonexistent as an issue as far as I am concerned. I think that to fight four years, to lose 20,000-plus Americans and to spend $50 billion in order to preserve a one-party dictator in South Vietnam is not a worthy objective for the United States.

PROFESSOR NUTTER: If that was trivial, then you really do have a problem. You started out saying that we should never have been there in the first place. But we went there and committed ourselves to self-determination back in the early '60s when precisely that kind of government—Diem's—was in power. The Diem government could hardly be considered a government that was more free than the present one. And so, by your reasoning, we have engaged ourselves in a horrible enterprise and lost not just your 20,000 men but 45,000 men, and cost ourselves billions and

125

billions of dollars for a totally trivial cause. That is an amazing thing to say if one goes back to see how many people were involved in making that commitment. It is a very, very sharp indictment of our entire country.

But it does not answer the question of what kind of solution we should get. We should get the kind of solution for which we made a commitment.

GENE LA ROCQUE, Center for Defense Information and United States Navy (retired): Professor Nutter, many of my colleagues have thought that the delay in reaching a peace agreement over the years was due to the constraints placed on the military. You alluded to that earlier. I wonder if you could tell us, sir, what constraints were placed on the military and whether they were a factor in delaying the peace agreement, from any period you choose, but particularly from '69 to '73.

PROFESSOR NUTTER: I can be very brief about the period '69 to '73. As I tried to say in one sentence of my presentation, military victory was simply ruled out in 1969 because it was inconceivable—given the history of the war, the circumstances, and all the rest—that the public would have supported what was necessary to get such a victory. And so I would say the constraints were quite necessary from the standpoint of public policy.

GILVEN SLONIM, The Oceanic Educational Foundation: Mr. Warnke, you have tended to sort of waffle over the strategic significance of this real estate we call Vietnam. Some in the audience may agree with you, others may not. But the question I would raise is this: In the event that you are proven wrong and there is strategic significance for the United States in Vietnam, does not our 1973 agreement put us in a better position to maintain a posture that attains our national goals insofar as areas external to our own continent are concerned?

MR. WARNKE: Well, I would suppose, sir, that the easy answer I would give is no. I don't think that who is in control in the lower righthand corner of the Indochinese peninsula matters one darn as far as American strategic posture is concerned. The only interest that we have had in Southeast Asia for some time has been to get out and to do so with a minimum of fuss. It doesn't make any difference in terms of bringing Soviet power closer to us, which is really the principal strategic concern of the United States. It has very little to do with our posture in the world, almost none. And in terms of commitment—and here, Dr. Nutter, I am afraid I have to agree with your restatement of my reasoning—I would have to say that getting into Vietnam was a cosmic mistake and that there is blame enough to go around. That blame has to be shared among Republicans and Democrats, among politicians, bureaucrats, journalists.

I think the *fact* we have to recognize at this point—that we made a mistake—is not inconsistent with our position as a great power. Fiorello LaGuardia was a great mayor, and he used to say, "When I make a mistake, it's a beaut." We made a mistake in Vietnam and it was a beaut. And I think whether the commitment was to President Thieu or to Premier Ky or to Diem or to Bao Dai, it was not a commitment that was worth our while, it was not a commitment that served the interests of the United States, and it was not a commitment that served the interest of the Vietnamese people. We should have recognized that years ago and, having recognized it, we should have terminated our involvement.

PROFESSOR NUTTER: Mr. Warnke is advocating, in essence, that we take the position in the world that amounts to saying, Yes, we have a commitment to our NATO allies, but when the crunch comes, we'll take a look at the situation and see whether we are going to honor the commitment. I submit that for the United States to take such a posture in the world would be faster suicide than any posture that Mr. Warnke has suggested that we have taken.

MR. WARNKE: What I would suggest is that our only commitment is to the security of the United States. Our NATO commitment is in the interest of the security of the United States. It is a clear commitment. It says that we will regard any attack on any NATO country as an attack on the United States. The SEATO agreement, to which South Vietnam is just a protocol member in a very ambiguous, cloudy situation, is by no means the equivalent of that commitment. By acting as if we regard our "commitment" to South Vietnam as being in the same category as our NATO obligation, we cheapen our NATO commitment and weaken our position in the world.

PROFESSOR NUTTER: Let me read again from the Tonkin Gulf Resolution, passed in our Congress in 1964, 504 votes to 2.

> The United States is, therefore, prepared, as the President determines, to take all necessary steps, including the use of armed force, to assist any member or protocol state of the Southeast Asia Collective Defense Treaty requesting assistance in defense of its freedom.

I cannot imagine a commitment more definite or specific than that one.

MR. WARNKE: It is a very clear resolution. Like all resolutions, it's subject to revocation. In fact, it *was* revoked just about a year ago. It should have been revoked several years ago.

That is exactly the issue we are debating tonight.

PROFESSOR NUTTER: But it was not revoked until a year ago.

MR. WARNKE: That is correct. What I am saying is that it should have been revoked earlier.

PROFESSOR NUTTER: But it *was* a commitment.

MR. WARNKE: That is the issue between us.

PROFESSOR NUTTER: But it was a *commitment.*

MR. WARNKE: It was a commitment subject to revocation.

PROFESSOR NUTTER: It was much firmer than any commitment we have made to NATO. Much firmer.

MR. WARNKE: It was not a treaty. It was a declaration that at that time—

PROFESSOR NUTTER: No, it was not a treaty. It was not passed by two-thirds of the Senate, but by the entire Congress—with only two dissenting votes. It was as deep a commitment as this country has ever made to the defense of any other—

MR. WARNKE: I am not denying the existence of the Tonkin Gulf Resolution. All I am saying is that we stuck with it too long. That is the issue. If you make a mistake, you are not condemned to live with it forever.

PROFESSOR NUTTER: No, you aren't. I quite agree with you, Paul—if you could have gotten the Congress to agree with you and to have revoked it in some sense. But Congress didn't. And therefore it was a commitment.

MR. WARNKE: I am not denying that. As I said there is blame enough to go around. I don't exonerate the Congress of the United States.

PROFESSOR NUTTER: I thought you were arguing that whenever we discover we have made a mistake in a commitment, we simply say, Sorry, boys, we made a mistake; it's too bad—

MR. WARNKE: And we do it collectively.

PROFESSOR NUTTER: —but we aren't going through with it because we've changed our minds.

MR. WARNKE: And we do it by the normal processes. That's correct.

MODERATOR GORALSKI: Gentlemen, thank you very much. You have given us some homework—Clark Clifford's article in 1969 and the Vietnamese peace terms for 1973.

Our thanks to you for being with us this evening—Warren Nutter, Paul Warnke, and distinguished panelists in the audience. [Applause.]

PART THREE
Two Journalists' Views

LECTURES

JOHN P. ROCHE

As one who has followed the negotiations in Vietnam with microscopic interest, first from within the government and then from outside, I must begin by congratulating the Hanoi politburo on one of the most spectacularly conducted exercises in political warfare the modern world has seen. Several volumes have been published about the abortive negotiations of the Johnson administration (of which Chester Cooper's *The Lost Crusade* is by far the best), but, alas, none makes the point that for years Ho Chi Minh and his colleagues played us like salmon. We were interested in negotiations to end the war on essentially a Korean or "stalemate" basis; they employed negotiations as a weapons system in the effort to destroy our will to maintain our Southeast Asian commitment.

Anyone who is optimistic about the outcome of present developments should learn caution, recalling that in 1954 Ho Chi Minh bitterly resented being forced by Moscow and Peking (then in tandem) to accept what was de facto a "two Vietnams" solution. The basis for this decision to downgrade Southeast Asia was a Soviet trade-off with France involving the latter's rejection of the European Defense Community. (Both the Soviet Union and the United States had their central focus on Europe; indeed, American involvement with the French in Indochina originated from what were seen as NATO imperatives.)

At any rate, despite the "Final Declaration," which everybody quotes but nobody signed, all that emerged from Geneva was bad news for the Viet Minh. Verbally "unification" of Vietnam was affirmed by the Communist powers, but the agreements actually signed at Geneva provided for regroupment of Viet Minh from the South to the North and conversely for regroupment of anti-Communists from North to South. Patently, regroupment and unification do not fit in the same logical universe: in effect, a "temporary" cold war boundary, like that between East and West Germany or North and South Korea, was drawn along the 17th parallel. (Subsequently the U.S.S.R. nominated both Vietnams for U.N. membership!)

To revert to the main theme, optimists should also recall that Ho Chi Minh, dismayed as he was at this betrayal by his "socialist brothers," simply went back to the drawing board. Ten years later Vietnam was back in the news. Today Pham Van Dong (who was at Geneva in 1954) probably views the cease-fire as Ho did the Geneva accord— a tactical retreat forced upon Hanoi by its self-centered Communist allies. What remains to be seen is whether Hanoi's resources and commitment to "unification" are adequate for another "liberation" scenario.

It is difficult to get the American people to realize that although negotiations have been in the air for a decade, the recent Paris accord represents the first step across the substantive threshold. To put it another way, up to now we have been dealing with negotiations about negotiations. But the Paris arrangements, though not really a "settlement," do incorporate *sub silentio* certain principles and reject others. It is clear to anyone who has followed this ballet that Hanoi has backed down at certain crucial points. It is thus preposterous to say that the same terms could have been achieved in 1968 or 1969. We are dealing with a set of familiar pieces: a cease-fire (proposed by President Johnson in his 1968 State of the Union Address), the "leopard skin map" (a modern adaptation of the feudal technique that, for example, in the Edict of Nantes gave the Huguenots a hundred fortified cities in Catholic France), a "coalition government," and the like. What is distinctive about the Kissinger-Tho accord is the arrangement of these pieces.

As I said, the United States was subjected to a superb Communist agitprop campaign on the subject of "negotiations." The governing maxim was set out candidly by Pham Van Dong to the late Bernard Fall as early as 1962: "Americans," Pham said, "do not like long inconclusive wars —and this is going to be a long inconclusive war."[1] Then, in 1965-67, we made a tragic strategic blunder which played into Ho Chi Minh's hand: we "Americanized" the war. Secretary of Defense Robert S. McNamara and his assorted "games" experts decided that it would be wasteful to spend a lot of useful energy training the South Vietnamese Army (ARVN). After all, it took almost two years to train the first competent Republic of Korea divisions, and in that time we could win the war all by ourselves. The United States, with its massive technological assets, would directly

[1] Bernard Fall, *Vietnam Witness, 1953-66* (New York: Praeger Publishers, 1966), p. 113.

force the North Vietnamese to desist from aggression; bombing would "punish" them. Once Ho and Vo Nguyen Giap, his military chief, knew that they were up against *real* Americans, they would cooperate with the chess players in the Pentagon and concede "mate in eight moves." I was personally convinced in the spring of 1965 that there were eminent men in the administration who were certain that the first time an American jet flew over Hanoi, Ho would come running out with a white flag. (Those who at this point suspect me of 20/20 hindsight are referred to my article, "The Liberals and Vietnam," in *The New Leader,* April 26, 1965.)

The "McNamara shortcut" seemingly had two admirable arguments in its favor: first, we could effectively ignore the condition of the Saigon government, and second, we could employ our air assets with a relatively light loss of American lives. The unfortunate consequence was that the ARVN was treated as an orphan and given essentially a spectator's role in the U.S.-Hanoi competition. (The order for M-16s, automatic rifles, for ARVN was not placed until the spring of 1968!)

My friend Amrom Katz of RAND tells me that, in California, pedestrians have an absolute right-of-way over drivers, but that before you start across the street you had better be certain that the car bearing down on you has California plates. In this sense, the McNamara shortcut (which of course was approved by President Johnson) required the cooperation of Ho Chi Minh. In the recently published *Cairo Documents,* Mohamed Heikal relates that in 1959 the Syrians and the Jordanians wanted Nasser to launch a limited war against Israel. Nasser's reply was succinct: "I am willing to carry out a limited war," the Egyptian President said, "but only if one of you gets me Ben Gurion's assurance that he too will limit it. For a war to be limited depends on the other side." [2]

Unfortunately Ho and Giap were never programmed by the Pentagon's game-theorists. They were determined to prevent the United States from fighting a cut-rate war. Down the Ho Chi Minh trail came the trained regiments of the North Vietnamese Army (PAVN) with the mission, not of defeating the United States on the ground, but of forcing the Americans to fight a ground war in full, costly visibility. To a considerable degree these troops were on a suicide mission, but when one appreciates that their goal was *political* rather than military, the "kill-ratio" loses much of its impact. We measured one thing, they measured another.

Let me insert a memorandum I wrote to President Johnson on March 27, 1967. It was occasioned by Ho Chi Minh's release of the letters between Johnson and himself, an act which puzzled the late President (who was born without an ideological bone in his body) and led him to ask me what I thought lay behind it. (I have not edited the memo except to delete references to some materials included as appendices.)

March 27, 1967

MEMORANDUM FOR
   The President
I have been following the negotiation sequence very

---

[2] Mohamed Heikal, *Cairo Documents* (Garden City, N.Y.: Doubleday and Co., 1973), pp. 27-28.

closely and have reached the conclusion that we are no longer fighting a "war" in Vietnam—we are fighting a "negotiation."

This is not intended as a cute play on words—on the contrary, it has serious consequences for American policy.

At the risk of boring you, let me set out the assumptions on which this is based:

1. Ho Chi Minh is not just a radical nationalist like Toure, Castro, or Sukarno. He is a dedicated Leninist, the last of the first generation of the Communist International.

2. He is therefore not a simple-minded Vietnamese chauvinist who, for example, will "not negotiate under pressure." I was in the Air Force too long to believe all I read about the effectiveness of bombing. But the view that Ho will not negotiate until we stop bombing is nonsense.

—it might be true of Castro, who is basically a romantic Latin fascist, a "petty-bourgeois sentimentalist" in Communist jargon;

—but Ho—like Lenin at the time of Brest-Litovsk— would negotiate in cold blood for whatever goals he considers realistic—even if bombs were coming down his chimney.

3. The behavior of a dedicated, intelligent Leninist is highly predictable. I never doubted that Khrushchev would pull the missiles out of Cuba in October 1962.

4. A good Leninist looks on the use of force as merely a variety of politics. He never adopts an inflexible "unconditional surrender" position, but is always ready to alter the timetable if the costs of overt aggression become too high.

5. On the basis of various statements that have been emerging from Hanoi over the past six months, as well

as articles in *Hoc Tap,* and other Communist organs in Hanoi, I am convinced that Ho knows that the road to victory in South Vietnam *by overt aggression* is closed.

6. He is therefore willing to shift from overt war to negotiations, with the latter in no way compromising his determination to someday "unify" Vietnam. Negotiations are a weapons system at which Ho is an expert (see his performance between the French and the Chinats from 1946-49 or his 1949-53 moves with the French).

7. This willingness to shift gears created trouble for Lenin and has undoubtedly created internal difficulties for Ho. My guess is that he released the exchange of letters to show the hard-liners he is still tough. There is probably a "negotiate-now" faction in Hanoi and he rhetorically disassociated himself from them.

8. But the real issue is Ho's authority: his capacity to free himself from factional control and be completely "opportunist"—in Lenin's use of the word, i.e., maintain the right to seize and utilize any opportunity that arises.

9. Assuming that Ho has adopted a tactic of negotiation (no Leninist looks on negotiations as valuable in themselves), but does not think *now* is the time to move, the release of the exchange of letters makes sense in terms of maintaining his freedom of maneuver.

10. Under what circumstances can we expect him to actually implement this tactic of negotiation?

At the worst possible time in terms of American internal unity—say on September 1, 1968. Recall that in dealing with the French in 1953, Ho waited until France was in a state of almost total political chaos over the European Defense Community to float his offer to negotiate.

11. What this comes down to is a rejection of the newspaper view that Hanoi is full of parochial primitives who do not "understand the United States."

Let us rather assume:

1) That they know exactly what they are doing;

2) That they are now out to win a negotiation;

3) That they recall both Panmunjon and two Genevas;

4) That they believe their maximum retrieval can be accomplished when the American people are really hurting and have a chance to bring real pressure directly on the presidential election;

5) That their present "insane" military operations are designed not to "win" the war, or to cut I Corps off from the rest of Vietnam, but simply to kill more Americans at *whatever cost* in North Vietnamese. To a dedicated old Bolshevik a weekly headline in the *Times* "U.S. Deaths Reach New All Time High" is worth 5,000 dead peasants from the PAVN.

6) That, in short, Ho is not counting on the peaceniks but on the isolationists in the United States and believes (correctly) that coffins are more significant propaganda than leaflets. And he also believes that we will not invade, really destroy, or try to liberate the DRV, so he can outwait us in his political sanctuary.

12. This is getting too long, and it may be fantasy, but I think we have to be prepared for such a contingency. In practice, it is not enough to have Governor Harriman ready to sit down anywhere, anytime. The key question is "What is he going to say?"

Suppose, sometime next year, Ho surfaces with a "Laotion solution"? Are we prepared to go for the principle of tripartite rule in SVN? Tripartism was a phony in Laos from the moment the 1962 agreement was signed, but it covered a *de facto* military partition which we and the Communists were prepared to live with.

When we say, therefore, that we are willing to go back to the 1962 Geneva agreement, we *mean* neutralization under great power guarantees, a stabilization.

But suppose Ho says, in the middle of a presidential campaign: "Fine, let's apply the 1962 Geneva principle to South Vietnam." The pressure to accept would be enormous, but acceptance would mean "coalition government" in Saigon, legitimation of the NLF, and break the back of our moral/military commitment.

Which, finally, accounts for the Saigon reaction to Ambassador Bunker. The South Vietnamese leaders are no dumber than those in Hanoi and they have good memories. They have seen the gallows (to paraphrase Dr. Johnson) and it has most wonderfully clarified their thought.

If you put yourself in Ky's shoes, and listened to some of your advisors relate matters of recent history in Asia, Ellsworth Bunker *could* easily be seen as the man who implemented Bobby Kennedy's policy of "appeasement" of Sukarno.

You would then probably ask the question: "Bobby Kennedy has come out for 'coalition,' Harriman was the architect of Laos, 1962, where does Bunker stand?" And you might well lie awake nights worrying about the "inscrutable Americans."

John P. Roche

This memorandum has been included because it establishes, I submit, my credentials as a critic of the negotiations process. (It is also revealing, I fear, as an index of the horrendous extent to which I fall under the bulls of excommunication recently pronounced on the Kennedy and Johnson administrations by Popes Henry Fairlie and David Halberstam.)

From the very outset, then, Hanoi was eager to negotiate on its own terms, but between 1964 and 1973 the North Vietnamese posture changed radically. In 1964, in an episode blown out of all proportions by the press when it came to light after Adlai Stevenson's death, Ho Chi Minh informed us through the United Nations that he would be pleased to meet our negotiator in Rangoon. Everything, he assured U.N. Secretary General U Thant, could be worked out so simply: the United States would agree to withdraw, would accept the position of the North Vietnamese, the program of the National Liberation Front of South Vietnam (the Viet Cong), and—presto—the war would be over.

Ho set no precondition for negotiations except the acceptance of the "Four and the Five," as they came to be known after full formulation in the spring of 1965. In blunt terms he agreed to accept our capitulation as a precondition for negotiating the modalities of surrender. Since the "Four and the Five" remained constants in the negotiating equation for some time, it might be well to set them out here.

HANOI'S FOUR POINTS:
Excerpts from a Speech by Pham Van Dong,
Premier of North Vietnam[3]
April 8, 1965

It is the unswerving policy of the Government of the Democratic Republic of Vietnam to strictly respect the 1954 Geneva Agreements on Vietnam, and to

---

[3] As reported by the Vietnamese News Agency, April 8, 1965.

correctly implement their provisions as embodied in the following points:

1. Recognition of the basic national rights of the Vietnamese people: peace, independence, sovereignty, unity and territorial integrity. According to the Geneva Agreements, the U.S. Government must withdraw from South Vietnam all U.S. troops, military personnel and weapons of all kinds, dismantle all U.S. military bases there, cancel its "military alliance" with South Vietnam. It must end its policy of intervention and aggression in South Vietnam. According to the Geneva Agreements, the U.S. government must stop its acts of war against North Vietnam, completely cease all encroachments on the territory and sovereignty of the Democratic Republic of Vietnam.

2. Pending the peaceful reunification of Vietnam, while Vietnam is still temporarily divided into two zones the military provisions of the 1954 Geneva Agreements on Vietnam must be strictly respected: the two zones must refrain from joining any military alliance with foreign countries, there must be no foreign military bases, troops and military personnel in their respective territory.

3. The internal affairs of South Vietnam must be settled by the South Vietnamese people themselves, in accordance with the programme of the South Vietnam National Front for Liberation, without any foreign interference.

4. The peaceful reunification of Vietnam must be settled by the Vietnamese people in both zones, without any foreign interference.

This stand unquestionably enjoys the approval and support of all peace and justice-loving Governments and peoples in the world.

The Government of the Democratic Republic of Vietnam is of the view that the above-expounded stand is the basis for the soundest political settlement of the Vietnam problem. If this basis is recognized, favourable conditions will be created for the peaceful settlement of the Vietnam problem and it will be possible to consider the reconvening of an international conference along the pattern of the 1954 Geneva Conference on Vietnam.

The Government of the Democratic Republic of Vietnam declares that any approach contrary to the above stand is inappropriate; any approach tending to secure a U.N. intervention in the Vietnam situation is also inappropriate because such approaches are basically at variance with the 1954 Geneva Agreements on Vietnam.

THE LIBERATION FRONT'S FIVE POINTS:
Excerpts from a Statement by the Central Committee of the South Vietnamese Liberation Front[4]
March 22, 1965

1. The United States imperialists are the saboteurs of the Geneva Agreements, the most brazen warmonger and aggressor and the sworn enemy of the Vietnamese people.

2. The heroic South Vietnamese people are resolved to drive out the U.S. imperialists in order to liberate South Vietnam, achieve an independent, democratic, peaceful and neutral South Vietnam, with a view to national reunification.

3. The valiant South Vietnamese people and the South Vietnam Liberation Army are resolved to ac-

---

[4] From a report by the Vietnamese News Agency, March 22, 1965.

complish to the full their sacred duty to drive out the U.S. imperialists so as to liberate South Vietnam and defend North Vietnam.

4. The South Vietnamese people express their profound gratitude to the wholehearted support of the peoples of the world who cherish peace and justice and declare their readiness to receive all assistance including weapons and all other war materials from their friends in the five continents.

5. To unite the whole people, to arm the whole people, continue to march forward heroically and be resolved to fight and to defeat the U.S. aggressors and the Vietnamese traitors.

After we began sustained bombing of the North in February 1965, the Hanoi agitprop division moved into high gear. "Stop the Bombing!" became the worldwide *mot d'ordre.* President Johnson, at Johns Hopkins University in April 1965, launched the only effective counterattack of his Vietnam ordeal when he called for "unconditional negotiations." This sounded good, but unfortunately it was soon overpowered by the amazing orchestration of anti-bombing propaganda that spread throughout the world and began to make a dent in the United States, notably on the college campuses. Johnson, whose bombing policy was motivated at least in part by a belief that it gave us a chip to play in negotiations (that is, you stop asking us to negotiate on the basis of the Four and the Five and we will stop bombing), found himself perplexingly confronted by a "world opinion" that seemed to make a moral distinction between high explosives delivered air mail and those sent parcel post. As far as Hanoi was concerned, it was money in the bank:

North Vietnam now added a bombing halt to its earlier negotiating preconditions.

At the risk of sounding cynical, let me say that I watched the American government's flailing efforts to launch negotiations with great skepticism. Walt Rostow's graphs were extremely persuasive in suggesting the degree to which we were "winning," but I wondered what Ho's graphs told him. Indeed, in a sardonic moment after a top level military briefing in Hawaii, I sent a back-channel message to the White House suggesting that Ho Chi Minh was the man who should get the briefing so he would know enough to quit. Fortunately I was out of reach, but Harry McPherson, special counsel to President Johnson, later told me the President was not amused.

For several years the North Vietnamese political warfare experts had a marvelous time. Kites would be flown in the most unlikely places: a Hanoi actor performing in some African nation would pointedly tell the French (or British, or Dutch, or . . .) second secretary at a cocktail party that the Four and the Five were not inscribed in tablets of stone, that maybe there was some room for maneuver. First, of course, the bombing must stop, but then, who knows? This would lead to a spasm in the Averell Harriman office, a small unit in the State Department charged with following up all chances for negotiations. Cables would fly off to Ft. Lamy, and inevitably, when the smoke cleared, there was nothing there. Except perhaps some headlines in the American press to the effect that, by our rigidity, we had thrown away another chance for peace.

In addition, North Vietnamese pronouncements were read with a textual passion worthy of a great Talmudist. I recall in the winter of 1967 the ubiquitous Pham Van Dong gave an interview to Harrison Salisbury of the *New York Times*. Salisbury quoted Pham as saying that the Four Points constituted "a" basis for settlement. Great excitement: obviously by the use of "a," Pham was opening up the field. (The Four Points had been previously dictated as "the" basis.) Just about the time the Talmudists had gotten their interpretive talents into motion, however, Pham issued a retraction, or a denial: he had said "the." "But comrade," to paraphrase one Talmudic whiz, "can it be a coincidence that the Hanoi censor cleared Salisbury's original dispatch complete with 'a'?" And on it went.

President Johnson and President Nixon were antipodal characters. Johnson, who needless to say hated the war, responded to criticism by frenzied activities designed to prove to the American people that he really did want peace. (To employ the current vocabulary of politics, Johnson's motto was "when in doubt, punt." Nixon, in contrast, operates on the maxim "when in doubt, fall on the ball.") He decided in the winter of 1965 that one way he could prove his bona fides to the people was to stage a peace extravaganza: he stopped the bombing on December 24, and immediately emissaries were practically shot out of cannons into the wide world to spread the tidings of American willingness to negotiate. The pause lasted 37 days. In substantive terms, its effect was pithily summed up by the late President when he noted that everywhere the Hanoi reply was the same: "———— you, Lyndon Johnson."

To avoid misunderstanding, let me state that I would have been delighted to have seen genuine negotiations. My reservations (as indicated in the memo above) were founded on my reading of Hanoi's view of the situation. From its vantage point, by its graphs, North Vietnam was *winning.* Thus Hanoi had absolutely no incentive to negotiate. Although the bombing was doing a good deal of damage, it was tolerable and stimulated both the Russians and Chinese Communists to substantial aid programs.

Sir Basil Liddell-Hart has observed that if Stalin had modernized Russia's road network in the inter-war period, the Nazis would have reached Moscow in six weeks. As it was, the very primitiveness of Soviet facilities bogged the Wehrmacht down. Bombing North Vietnam was analogous: provided we avoided saturation bombing and dike-busting, targets were soon in short supply. The notion of holding an economy hostage might make some sense in the case of, say, Japan, but it was absurd in this context. Mining the harbors made a great deal of military sense, but Johnson outlawed it on the ground that it could trigger intervention by Peking or Moscow. (The fact that Mr. Nixon got away with it in 1972, by the way, is no proof that Johnson was wrong in 1965-68: the dynamics of international relations are radically different today from those of only eight years ago.)

This rambles a bit, but art does reflect life and Vietnamese reality was and remains nothing if not rambling. Without trying to write a precis of the war, let me ask the question: Under what circumstances would Hanoi have felt it to be in its interest genuinely to negotiate? The answer, of course, is when it felt threatened—or, alternatively, when it appeared that a viable regime was emerging in the South, and negotiations could forestall the consolidation of power in Saigon. So long as the United States and Hanoi were fighting a private war under restricted ground rules (no invasion of the North and the Cambodian sanctuaries, no bombing of the dikes or city-busting, et cetera), Ho Chi Minh had no reason to feel threatened. True, in 1967 the Republic of Vietnam had adopted a constitution, held elections, and generally moved towards a representative form of government. But President Thieu's army was still an orphan and realists in Hanoi had no reason to suppose that, once the Americans went home, the Saigon government could last a week under sustained military assault.

Right on into 1968, then, Hanoi played negotiating games. As American casualties mounted, and particularly with the Tet offensive being billed as a big Communist victory, it seemed only a matter of time before the Americans, like the French before them, would "lose the war at home" and vanish across the seas. One intelligence report quoted a high North Vietnamese official as cheerfully announcing at a diplomatic function that he would be delighted to negotiate with the Americans—on what music would be played for their retreat. Obviously in a jovial mood, he offered to provide the bands and a red carpet strewn with rose petals. After President Johnson's dramatic announcement of March 31, 1968, Hanoi was shrewd enough to pick up the offer to meet—and suggested Phnom Penh as the locus!

As usual we came out of the episode looking like clumsy clowns: in an expansive mood Johnson had said he would go anywhere, anytime to negotiate. Now we were forced, for perfectly sensible reasons, to turn down a series of cities, to rush around looking for counterproposals to prove our sincerity, and eventually to settle for the inevitable Paris (which the Vietnamese had probably decided on in the first place—they like Paris). Delegations were appointed and set forth upon their labors, but the Hanoi team insisted that no substantive talks could occur until a total bombing halt had been declared. At this point Johnson dug in his heels and, despite the sometimes tearful pleas of Democratic politicians working for the candidacy of Vice President Humphrey, refused to budge until the other side came up with some specific pay-offs on its side of the hill.

Richard Whalen, in *Catch the Falling Flag,* casts his paranoidal eye on Johnson's decision to stop all bombing virtually on election eve and declares it an "ambush." This is an insult to the late President—not just to his sense of obligation to the nation, but to his superb talent as an ambusher. When L.B.J. set out to ambush somebody, they stayed ambushed. The actual sequence of events was quite different. The President had instructed Averell Harriman and Cyrus Vance in Paris that the bombing would not stop until North Vietnam made a flat commitment to (1) respect the Demilitarized Zone (DMZ), (2) stop shelling and rocketing the cities of the South, and (3) ignore U.S. aerial reconnaissance of the North. The Hanoi representatives circled the bush, but began to make more friendly noises. These impressed Ambassador Harriman, who wanted to move ahead rapidly in the early fall, but by that time the President had come to suspect that Harriman's top priority was Humphrey's election. "I want it carved in concrete," the President told me—and Hanoi was not about to comply.

Meanwhile some other players got into the action: first the Soviet Union, which took a dim view of Richard Nixon as President of the United States, and second, the Saigon government, which after Humphrey's Salt Lake City speech reached the perfectly understandable conclusion that Nixon was its candidate. Although on its face the Salt Lake City speech adhered to the Johnson parameters on Vietnam, it was accompanied by extensive press backgrounding to the effect that Humphrey, if elected, would abandon the "rigidities" of the Johnson years. (Anna Chennault's role as intermediary between the Republican party and Saigon has probably been exaggerated because, on self-interest grounds, the Thieu government would have been moronic not to back Nixon—and that government included some extremely intelligent men.)

In the end, these late arrivals cancelled each other out. The Soviet Union obtained solid assurances from Hanoi about the three point "understanding," on October 31 the President announced a total bombing halt and the beginning of substantive talks, and in the next few days Saigon blew the whole package sky-high. Recall again that—contrary to common belief—Hanoi had not at this point agreed to peace. It had simply agreed to stop negotiating about nego-tiating and to begin substantive talks. The only thing that was "blown" at this point was the opportunity to get down to business; in January, after the shape of the table and other arcane matters had been arranged, the "two sides, four parties" finally held their first formal meeting.

To summarize, then, as Richard Nixon entered the White House, Hanoi's *substantive* negotiating position was essentially unchanged. Over the years, the "Four and the Five" points had been refined into two starkly simple demands: (1) get all American forces out of Indochina, and (2) bust the government of the Republic of Vietnam, that is, destroy the fragile legitimacy of President Thieu's administration. The technique for achieving the second was the patented Communist formula for a takeover: a "coalition government"—not even a coalition including Thieu (as the Soviet Union used in Poland in 1945 when it permitted the London Polish government-in-exile to participate in a brief coalition), but one from which the elected President was specifically excluded.

The key to what has happened in the four subsequent years lies in one concept: Vietnamization. Actually it was Secretary of Defense Clark Clifford who initiated this policy, which amounted to de-Americanizing the war, in the last year of the Johnson administration. There were some of us who had been struggling for it under the rug for years, though without perceptible impact. On May 1, 1967 for example, I sent the President a memo (known to a few insiders as the "pneumonia memo"). Since my memos seem to be among the few unpublished items in the literature on Vietnam, I trust I may be excused for partially remedying that gap.

May 1, 1967

MEMORANDUM FOR
     The President
I don't know whether it makes me a hawk, a dove, or a penguin, but for a year or more I have had very serious doubts about our Vietnamese strategy.

I don't think we have taken a "hard" enough line on what is really required to achieve our objectives.

—I have no objection to bombing North or South so long as we realize that air power, in anything short of a nuclear context, is merely *mobile artillery*.

—What has distressed me is the notion (expressed time and again by the Air Force boys) that air power would provide a *strategic* route to victory;

—And the parallel assumption that by bombing the North we could get a cut-rate solution in the South and escape from the problems of building a South Vietnamese army.

I raised the question of the rebuilding of ARVN in several memos to you last fall. Regrettably, I could write the same memos today. There are about 650,000 South Vietnamese under arms (in various categories), but we have still not done the job we did in Korea. Or even started to do it.

And the lead-time remains the same—stretched into the future—and the same argument seems to be employed against reforming ARVN—namely, that it will require too much lead-time.

As you know by now (I hope), I am not intellectually or temperamentally inclined to play "Rover Boy with the Joint Chiefs." But I do know that if I were a professional military man, I would be making demands upon you that would be contrary to the political strategy you have laid down for Vietnam.

Essentially the very concept of "limited war" runs against the grain of a dedicated military professional.

—And I don't *blame* him for this in the slightest. He is not trained, or paid, to think about political considerations.

(In this connection, I had a very interesting talk with General Clay in Bad Godesberg. I asked him why we had not insisted on land access to Berlin in 1945. He said that F.D.R. had not so instructed Ike, and that anyone who blamed Ike for the decision (me among others) was a "dumb son of a bitch." Ike, he said, was paid to make military decisions—and made one. Those of us who didn't like the decision, should blame F.D.R. and Truman. I am not in the habit of admitting that I am a "dumb son of a bitch," but in fact Clay was absolutely right.)

The simple military answer to the war in Vietnam is "destroy the enemy," and they could do a very good job of it if you turned them loose, doubled or tripled our commitment, authorized nuclear weapons, etc., etc.

In essence, they are like doctors who have a cure for pneumonia but not for a common cold—they therefore have a vested interest in the patient *getting* pneumonia.

To all of this you can correctly say "So what?" So let me try to set out what seems to me the outline of an effective strategy.

1. Our problems in the South, while sponsored and buttressed from the North, cannot be solved *in* the North unless we are prepared to abandon the strategy of limited war.

2. Specifically, we must win the war on the ground *in* the South. Ky and others have advocated an "Inchon landing" around Dong Hoi. Perhaps they should meditate on Anzio rather than Inchon—the analogy, in my judgment, is far more exact. Even by MACV's figures (which I profoundly mistrust—see my note to Walt at Tab 1), only a small percentage of the PAVN is in the panhandle.

3. At the risk of sounding banal, the war *in* the South can be won either by one to two million United

States troops or by 500-750,000 United States troops and a *well-trained ARVN.*

4. The key to "pacification" is *not* "winning the hearts and minds of the peasantry." All they want is peace and quiet. The key to pacification is the capacity to pacify, i.e., to beat the hell out of the guerrillas and thereby convince the peasants that the VC is a loser. Like others in the world, peasants love a winner, and are much too smart to pick a winner by reading one of Zorthian's seven billion leaflets.

5. The decision to win the war in the South does not necessarily involve cessation of bombing. But I would suggest that a utility study of bombing should accompany it. When I was in Saigon, I asked a high ranking Air Force officer who was two sheets to the wind why they had flown 350 sorties the day before. He said: "We have to fly 1.2 sorties per plane per day—weather permitting. Last week we were down to 1.16, but yesterday brought it up. The goddamned Navy was up to 2.25 last week."
There may be something to this, but more fundamentally the problem is that the Air Force does not *want* to do the job that needs doing. For example, in South Vietnam the most useful *mobile artillery* are helicopters and prop aircraft (the A-1 for example). Every time an Air Force General sees a prop-plane, he has an aesthetic shudder: he wants jets—*beautiful jets.* Jets are beautiful, but they are lousy mobile artillery in terms of close ground support.

6. Finally, the constant pressure to *do something* must be resisted. Sometimes the only thing on the shelf worth buying is *time.* Assuming as I do that nothing in the limited war range will force Hanoi to negotiate (and that total war is out of the question), we have a force in Vietnam that can buy time and hope-

fully do something with it, namely, make ARVN into an army.

John P. Roche

The fact is that until Clark Clifford became secretary of defense (March 1, 1968) nobody in a position to implement policy paid the slightest attention to Vietnamization. Perhaps I should exclude Secretary of State Dean Rusk, to whom— at the President's request—I sent a copy of this memo. The result was a long private conversation in which it became clear to me that Rusk shared my misgivings but, always meticulous in these matters, felt that the question was in McNamara's jurisdiction. The President, who made no substantive comment at the time, mentioned the memo seven months later, in December, when he said to me: "Maybe I'm going to do something that will make you happy. All they want is more of the same and I'm not going to give it to them. They're going to have to live with what they got —that common cold—and waste some of their valuable time training Viets." By the time I had figured out that "they" was the Joint Chiefs of Staff and the subject was training ARVN, he had changed the subject.

No, it was the Nixon administration which finally reversed the tide, and did so in one of the most daring gambles in military history. The new President, realizing fully that the source of our Vietnam malaise was American casualties, not an upsurge of pacifism, decided to pull out the "teeth"—that is, the American combat troops—and compensate for their relief by the overpowering use of tactical air power. And he decided to make an army out of ARVN, or at least do everything in our power to give Saigon the capability of self-defense.

He also decided, when the appropriate moment appeared, to hit the Cambodian sanctuaries and, more important, to cut off the Communist supply line from the port of Sihanouk-ville. Those opposing this action had always downplayed the significance of the Cambodian port; yet when the balance was finally figured, it appeared that even supporters of action had drastically underestimated the logistical importance of the "Sihanouk Trail." (The Department of Defense, for example, was low by over 50 percent!) Cambodia was in fact, not a state, but a gun-running syndicate which issued postage stamps.

The temptation to make this into a history of the Vietnam war must be resisted. Our concern is narrower: the effect of Vietnamization on negotiations.

Unlike Jane Fonda and other similarly equipped authorities on Indochina, the leaders of the Dang Lao Dong—the North Vietnamese Communist party—are not under the illusion that 95 percent of the population of South Vietnam dreams of "liberation" from the alleged "police state" in Saigon. True, the South Vietnamese are war-weary, but they know the difference between a somewhat corrupt, somewhat authoritarian, somewhat inefficient government struggling up the ladder towards representative government and the ideological deep-freezer in the North. Thus Vietnamization, in the eyes of the Hanoi politburo, must have seemed like much more of a long-term threat than half a million American soldiers. This sent them back to the drawing board and what emerged was a new version of the classic "talk-fight" strategy.

The theory was that Vietnamization had to be utterly discredited in American and South Vietnamese eyes. The method was, of all things, a conventional invasion of the South complete with tanks and heavy artillery. Once the shock of surprise was over, the enormity of Giap's error became apparent: a T-54 is a formidable hunk of armor, but deploying tanks without air cover is another way of giving them away. A conventional invasion, to put it differently, was the one thing the Americans could easily handle. Had Giap deployed his manpower in Phase II guerrilla operations, there would have been real problems, but apparently he has a fixation on set-piece battles.

The invasion did tear things up, but An Loc held, and Quang Tri was retaken, and ARVN fought. In another era the American media would have treated the defenders of An Loc, who were taking 5,000 artillery and rocket rounds a day at the peak of the siege, as heroic figures. As it was, the siege was handled in a rather rancid fashion, with heavy emphasis on the destruction of the town and the implication that if ARVN would stop defending it so stubbornly, there would be a lot less damage to innocent civilians. However, to those who were watching the important index, ARVN's performance indicated that our training program was working.

Also, Mr. Nixon took some initiatives of his own in the "talk-fight" scenario. First, he accused the North Vietnamese of violating the 1968 "understandings" and cancelled the bombing halt, and second, he mined the harbors of North

Vietnam. This was done against a background of visits to Peking and Moscow, where the President was greeted with far more warmth than would have been the case on the average American campus. (As a Secret Service friend once told me, "We always like state visits to Communist countries. They really turn the crowds out and you don't have to worry about a thing: nobody gets shot there except on orders.") The net result of this combination of actions was that Hanoi must have begun to feel quite lonely. Furthermore, as American troop strength dropped, the Communist demand for American withdrawal lost more and more of its utility. Le Duc Tho's task now centered on one objective: the United States must be forced somehow to break the back of the Thieu government.

On the surface, Le Duc Tho had some things going for him. The year 1972 was supposed to be an election year in the United States, the American people were tired of the war, and with a little help from antiwar forces, Thieu could be billed as the "obstacle to peace" who was single-handedly keeping the war going. (It got a bit confusing: Thieu, long featured as a U.S. puppet, now turned up with Nixon on strings.) However, the Democratic party waived its right seriously to contest the presidency, and Le Duc Tho had to continue his dialogue with Henry Kissinger.

It appears that Hanoi—under pressure from both Peking and Moscow—broke the ice on October 9 when it dropped the demand for Thieu's removal and replacement by a coalition government. As a fig leaf, the frustrated PRG (whose leaders in Paris were openly accusing Hanoi, Moscow and Peking of selling them down the Mekong) was offered membership in a tripartite National Council for National Reconciliation and Concord. To Saigon this "administrative structure," as it was originally called, still smacked of coalition government (in Vietnamese the phrases are very similar) and eventually that term was dropped.

The real sticking points, once Le Duc Tho had accepted "two Vietnams" *in principle,* were the modalities of the cease-fire and the prisoner issue. Hanoi's proposal for a 250-man peace-keeping force was patently a bad joke, particularly given the presence in South Vietnam of perhaps 150,000 North Vietnamese troops. Saigon was justifiably unsettled by the fact that the cease-fire left them in place, but Thieu's concerns could be offset by an effective policing mechanism—to say nothing of the continued presence of U.S. air power in Thailand and the Seventh Fleet in the Tonkin Gulf (in effect, the fleet constitutes an island we hold off the North Vietnamese coast).

As far as prisoners were concerned (American POWs aside), the issue was one of definition. Was the friendly neighborhood Communist who had chucked a grenade into a restaurant a "political prisoner"? Or a common murderer? (This question is going to plague us for some time. In that spirit I would suggest to the antiwar militants that their Vietnamese definition is fungible, that is, if the friendly neighborhood Viet Cong guerrilla is a "political prisoner," so is the Arab terrorist in Israel, or, for that matter, the black Muslims who recently killed members of a rival sect in Washington.) Le Duc Tho's strategy in October was clearly one of leaving everything as vague as possible and getting the Americans to sign on the dotted line.

At this point, late October, I suspect that an understandably jubilant Henry Kissinger went beyond his brief when, on the 26th, he announced that "we believe peace is at hand." Although he hedged his bet by noting that there were some unresolved details, the Communists instantly began an orchestration demanding instant signature. It depends on what you mean by an unresolved detail: the difference between a 250-man force and one of 3,300? the existence or nonexistence of the DMZ? the definition of terrorists as POWs?

In any event, perhaps in the belief that the President would be forced by American opinion to leave such details unresolved, Le Duc Tho began stone-walling and accusing the United States of reneging on prior agreements. Mr. Nixon in return flatly announced, on October 29, that we would not play, that he would not "allow an election deadline or any other kind of deadline to force us into an agreement which would be only a temporary peace and not a lasting peace." The election passed quietly and Kissinger returned to Paris on November 20 to iron out the details. Meanwhile, to prepare the Thieu government for the day it would have to handle its own defense, the United States rushed equipment to Saigon.

There are those who claim that Hanoi's hardening posture in November and December arose from an internal fight between the politburo's "hawks" and "doves," with the "hawks" temporarily gaining ascendancy. Lacking second sight, I am not competent to evaluate that contention, but the fact is that Le Duc Tho proved extremely obdurate about details, particularly the question of the DMZ. Symbolically, he had a point—as did Saigon, which had the DMZ very much on its mind: the DMZ is the clearest overt recognition of the existence of two Vietnams. After all, unless Korea is the model, one does not carve a demilitarized zone across the middle of a nation which is abstractly on the road to unification. And Korea is not the model Hanoi had in mind.

It is, I think, fair to say that over the past quarter of a century I have not been known as an admirer of Richard M. Nixon. However, I never made the error of underestimating his intelligence or of overlooking his renown as a poker player. Indeed, I date the demoralization of the antiwar movement to January 25, 1972, when—after being denounced far and wide in the media for his rigidity and unwillingness to negotiate—he flashed his hole card on nationwide television: he was negotiating secretly with Hanoi and had, in fact, submitted to Le Duc Tho via Henry Kissinger an eight-point peace program. Even Anthony Lewis was slowed down a bit—though only momentarily.

In December 1972, the President obviously decided that enough was enough and on the 18th the planes took off again for the North. Probably the B-52 strikes on Hanoi and Haiphong performed a useful military function, but my hunch is that their purpose went far beyond that. What the bombing campaign did was vividly demonstrate to the North Vietnamese that (1) the antiwar movement in the United States was dead, and (2) the Soviet Union and Communist China had left them to their fate. To my knowledge, no top Soviet official made any comment (*Tass* issued a low-level condemnation), and Chou En-lai merely observed to an American reporter that the bombing would "adversely affect" U.S.-Peking relationships. Hanoi, in short, learned the hard way that it was cold out there. On December 30 the President was able to announce that bombing above the 20th parallel had stopped and that the Kissinger-Tho meetings would resume on January 8, 1973. We all know the outcome.

As I suggested earlier, anyone who is optimistic about Vietnam should be instantly sent off for psychiatric observation. Yet, it is apparent that the terms of the cease-fire of 1973 are a quantum jump beyond any accord that could have been reached in 1968 or 1969. What President Nixon did was to develop a "talk-fight" strategy of his own and pursue it with single-minded dedication. Like President Eisenhower, who threatened to use nuclear weapons to end the Korean War, Nixon realized that the Hanoi politburo was not a branch of the Fellowship of Reconciliation. But unlike Eisenhower, whose immense prestige protected him from hostile domestic opinion, President Nixon had to manage his "talk-fight" campaign against a background of public and congressional enmity.

The cold-blooded use of military power to obtain political objectives is never a pleasant thing to watch. For understandable, indeed admirable, reasons the citizens of a free society and their elected representatives in Congress find "carpet bombing" repugnant, particularly in a twilight war against a small nation. What the critics of Nixon's strategy fail to take into consideration is that the Hanoi regime (a "grotesque dwarf" in Reinhold Niebuhr's vivid phrase) is dominated by as brilliantly ruthless an elite as the Communist movement has ever produced. What the President had to do was convince this elite that its national interest required serious negotiations. Once that was accomplished, as I noted in my memo to President Johnson, Hanoi would negotiate "with bombs coming down their chimneys." They did.

Achieving the cease-fire was, as the Duke of Wellington would have put it, "a close run thing"—what with Congress and the media constantly mounting pressure for virtually any means of extrication from the struggle. What the future holds, God only knows, but, as a primitive, liberal cold warrior, I personally am glad that—like John F. Kennedy and Lyndon B. Johnson before him—Richard Nixon does not consider American honor to be a bargain-basement commodity. The Paris accords, *if successfully implemented,* do constitute the fundaments of "peace with honor."

CLAYTON FRITCHEY

There is a lot to be said for postmortems, for that is how we learn about many things, especially crimes. So we are indebted to the American Enterprise Institute for sponsoring this examination of U.S. policy in Vietnam, and Southeast Asia in general. After all the sacrifices Americans have made in that region it would be a pity if we did not learn something from the experience, and the only way we can learn is by looking back, not in a spirit of recrimination, but in the hope of discovering where we went wrong. The process may be painful, but if we do not face up to it, we may be condemned to repeating it.

We continue to be so involved in the war and in the new cease-fire that it will be difficult for some time to avoid the temptation of political partisanship in discussing it. Nevertheless, discussion will be largely a waste of time if it is approached in that spirit. These pious thoughts may not seem suitable for one who, like myself, has been identified with Democratic administrations. I want to assure you, however, that I could not feel less partisan than I do about Vietnam and Asia in general. Although I served in the State Department and at the United Nations under the late President Lyndon Johnson, the first column I wrote over seven years ago was sharply critical of his military escalation in Vietnam. Looking back, I would say I wrote just as many critical columns about Mr. Johnson's conduct of the war as I have about Mr. Nixon's.

Also, I might say in passing that Mr. Johnson did not like it, and he let me know he did not. On one occasion, which I hope to write about at more length some day, he complained that he didn't think he was getting a fair shake from the more liberal columnists and commentators. He pointed out all he had done for civil rights and civil liberties and called attention to his Great Society. He felt that all this was being lost sight of by the liberals because of their preoccupation with the war. I readily conceded that he had advanced many liberal causes, but then I drew a tremulous breath, and said, "But, sir, what would President Lincoln's standing be today if he had been right on everything except the Civil War?" Mr. Johnson, I must report, was not noticeably amused.

In any case, our Vietnam policy—and the larger Asian policy from which it evolved—has never really been a partisan matter. The disappointing American crusade to make Asia and the Far East safe for democracy began under my old boss, Harry Truman, and has been carried on by two Democrats—John F. Kennedy and Lyndon Johnson—and two Republicans—General Eisenhower and President Nixon. There is plenty of blame for everybody, including the incumbent. Nevertheless, the incumbent is likely to get good marks from history, not because he fought the war better than his predecessors, but because he ended it—or, at least, ended America's involvement in it.

Beyond that, however, history is likely to recognize that he did something even more important: he finally ended America's long holy war against Asian communism and, simultaneously, launched a new era of coexistence and cooperation. If this leads, as it may, to a generation or more of peace, Mr. Nixon could end up occupying an enviable place in history. His critics no doubt will complain that his change of policy was made belatedly, grudgingly, and after years of unnecessary expenditures. But he did it, which is more than can be said of his predecessors in the White House.

Despite his shows of belligerence and his reassurances of fidelity to old allies in Southeast Asia, Mr. Nixon appears to be on the verge of repositioning the United States, not as an Asian mainland force but as the great Pacific power that it essentially is. That is America's proper role. Vast as the Pacific is, there is little question that the United States can preside over it unchallenged, without undue effort and without risk of war. In that immense domain, which reaches to the shores of both Asia and Southeast Asia, the United States has the key bases, the only strategic air force and the only great navy. Also, for the time being, it is the area's only advanced nuclear power.

President Nixon, in short, is retreating to a position of true strength, which should permit mainland Asia to evolve in its own way without jeopardizing the vital interests of the United States. In pulling the last of our troops out of Vietnam, Mr. Nixon is at last heeding the admonition of his old boss, President Eisenhower, not to engage in a land war in Asia.

However good our intentions originally may have been, the long crusade to make Asia safe for democracy has been a dismal failure. When that effort began after the end of World War II, there was at least a semblance of representative government in some of the countries that we were going to save, but today—five U.S. Presidents later—they have all become dictatorships, mostly run by generals. What a sad roll call it makes: South Vietnam, South Korea, Thailand, Cambodia, Laos, Taiwan. Even old friends and allies like the Philippines and Pakistan have gone totalitarian. The only new democracy to emerge in all of the East and Near East is Bangladesh—which, alas, emerged only over the opposition of the United States.

Politically, Mr. Nixon has chosen a good moment to act decisively, for even notable hawks like Senator Henry Jackson (Democrat, Washington) are now applauding the President's move toward an Asian détente. So if Mr. Nixon feels he needs a domestic green light, he has it. Once he is completely out of the Chinese and Vietnamese civil wars, and once the United States is again prudently postured in the Pacific, the President can turn his full attention to achieving his generation of peace, which calls for more than mere tranquillity in Asia.

167

There are signs that Mr. Nixon himself feels that our preoccupation with Vietnam has led us to neglect other regions of the world. He has just said, for instance, that this will be the "year of Europe." Simultaneously he sent a message to the Organization of American States pledging "priority attention" for Latin America. Conditions are especially propitious in Europe for solving or at least reducing old postwar problems. This, in turn, ought to help the United States and Russia make further progress in their efforts to limit strategic arms.

On balance then, the *world* outlook is relatively relaxed, but that does not mean the *local* outlook is also good. All signs point to a continuation of local conflicts in many parts of the world, not least in Vietnam itself. As I have indicated, Mr. Nixon may have arranged things so that the ultimate resolution in Vietnam will not greatly matter insofar as geopolitics or the vital interests of the United States are concerned. But it would be foolhardy to believe that he has actually arranged what he calls "peace with honor"—which, freely translated, means preservation of the government of President Nguyen Van Thieu.

The Nixon administration's justification for prolonging the war so long was that it felt obliged to improve the chances of South Vietnam's government to maintain itself in power. It insists that it has succeeded in this, but the case is not convincing. After Hanoi's costly Tet offensive in 1968, according to the White House and Pentagon, the North Vietnamese army was virtually wiped out, its best fighting units annihilated. When the Nixon administration came to power in 1969, there was not an organized enemy division in South Vietnam. Thieu's forces occupied nearly all of the South, the Viet Cong was reported on its last legs and, because of the reputed success of the U.S. "pacification" program, the people of South Vietnam were said to be solidly behind the Thieu government. In addition, the DMZ at the 17th parallel (dividing the North and South) had not then been breached. Cambodia, largely controlled by the Communists today, was then a neutral country.

Now, four years later, North Vietnam's rebuilt army is so strong that it would have conquered South Vietnam last spring had not the U.S. come to the rescue with all the power it had available. Further, the new cease-fire allows Hanoi to keep a minimum of 145,000 heavily armed troops in South Vietnam. The Viet Cong, moribund in 1969, is now to be the recognized government in many areas of the South. Indeed, Viet Cong officials have already started arriving in Saigon to participate in organizing the future of the South, which would have been unthinkable four years ago.

Had the U.S. withdrawn in 1969, Thieu would not have had to accept the present partition of his domain, nor would he have been endangered by an enemy-dominated Cambodia on his western border. It may be said that Thieu's army is larger and better equipped now than it was in 1969; but Hanoi's regrouped army demonstrated last spring that it could still overpower the South Vietnamese, regardless of their numbers.

In estimating Thieu's present chances of survival, it is useful to recall that the reason the United States intervened with ground forces in 1965 was that South Vietnam was collapsing internally, although North Vietnam then had no forces in the South. Today, with Hanoi's crack divisions on the scene and the Viet Cong getting a share of the government, is it possible to believe that Thieu has either a good or improved chance of survival? Hanoi will have little incentive to repudiate the cease-fire, for in its wake Thieu's army will probably melt away in the coming months. The desertion rate is already enormous.

Four years ago, South Vietnam had at least the appearance of a going democracy. Thieu had just been elected President in an election that Lyndon Johnson certified was on the level. Since then the government has degenerated into a military dictatorship, with thousands of political prisoners held in torture camps. The nation's National Assembly is a joke; even the locally elected hamlet chiefs have been supplanted by Thieu's followers. These are precisely the conditions that led to the downfall of former President Diem and brought about the intervention of U.S. armed forces.

It would be the final irony of America's intervention in Vietnam if, in the wake of the Washington-Hanoi cease-fire agreement, North Vietnam should end up dominating not only South Vietnam but most of Indochina as well. Such an outcome is by no means unlikely.

Before Indochina was split up by the 1954 Geneva Agreement, it consisted of Vietnam (North and South) plus Cambodia and Laos. The latter two became independent, supposedly neutral countries after the French were defeated by Ho Chi Minh's nationalist forces. Today, as a result of the American invasion of Cambodia in May 1970, which dragged Cambodia into the Vietnamese war, the future of that poor, shattered nation, now overrun by the Communists, is even more uncertain than that of the Saigon government under President Thieu. General Lon Nol's regime in Phnom Penh could easily fall before Thieu's.

Cambodia is an excruciating example of what can happen to a bystander country when, through no fault of its own, it gets caught up in a war which for years it has tried to avoid. Until Prince Norodom Sihanouk was overthrown in March 1970, Cambodia managed to maintain its neutrality, even though it sometimes had to blink at the presence of Communist troops on its long border with South Vietnam. It was the claimed need to wipe out these border sanctuaries that President Nixon used as his public justification for invading Cambodia in the spring of 1970. The alleged object of the American action was to smash the Communist forces in Cambodia, capture COSVN (supposedly the secret military nerve center of the enemy), support the new military government of General Lon Nol (which ousted Prince Sihanouk) and speed U.S. withdrawal from the war by fatally wounding the enemy.

Today, two-and-a-half years later, it all seems like a nightmare. The enemy was never found, nor was the fabled COSVN. Instead, the North Vietnamese swept over Cambodia and now occupy two-thirds or more of its territory. General Nol's authority is confined to Phnom Penh and a few other population centers. Meanwhile, the entire nation has been so bombed and scorched that a third of the population is homeless. In the midst of this, General Lon Nol ditched the constitution, disbanded the Assembly and turned Cambodia into a military dictatorship. Such is the present status of the country that, in the words of Senator Mike

Mansfield, the majority leader, used to be "an oasis in a war-torn Indochina."

Nonetheless, on November 15, 1971, 18 months after the invasion, Nixon was still saying that "Cambodia is the Nixon doctrine in its purest form." He also said, on December 10, 1970: "The quarter-billion-dollar aid program for Cambodia is, in my opinion, probably the best investment in foreign assistance that the United States has made in my lifetime." The Cambodian generals who have reportedly pocketed so many of these millions through graft and corruption would undoubtedly agree.

The North Vietnamese responded to the U.S. invasion of Cambodia by training and arming an ever-growing force of Cambodian insurgents, generally known as the Khmer Rouge. Since 1970, this hardy guerrilla force has increased from 3,000 to more than 30,000, and recently has been carrying on most of the fighting against Lon Nol's feckless army, leaving the North Vietnamese free to strike at South Vietnam.

There were those who laughed when Prince Sihanouk, from his refuge in Peking, said last December: "The government of the United States will see, in a not-too-distant future, the installation in Phnom Penh of the royal government under the aegis of the National United Front of Cambodia.[1] This means Sihanouk, backed by the Communists.

During the uncertainty of the off-again-on-again Washington-Hanoi accord, the only reliable administration spokesman was Henry Kissinger, in spite of the doubts raised by his premature heralding of peace last October. Professor John

---

[1] Letter from Sihanouk to *New York Times,* December 1, 1971.

Roche, like many others, thinks Dr. Kissinger exceeded his instructions—and went beyond his mandate from the President—in reaching the October agreement with the North Vietnamese. The truth is that Mr. Nixon's brilliant negotiator was telling it like it was at that time. But he remained loyally silent, privately as well as publicly, when the President, under pressure from Nguyen Van Thieu, abruptly pulled back from the accord.

The probability is that Dr. Kissinger will leave the administration when John Connally becomes the next secretary of state, as I expect he will. Meanwhile, however, the President still needs Kissinger badly, and so the White House has been trying to deflate the reports of a rift between the foreign affairs adviser and his boss.

The President's special counsel, Charles Colson, has made a remarkable statement, obviously with Nixon's approval, specifically denying any strain or misunderstanding between Dr. Kissinger and the President. It's all just a "full-blown myth," Colson says, "born in the Washington-Georgetown cocktail circuit." Elaborating on what is clearly to be the official White House version of the alleged rift, Colson accuses the press and television of "elevating this piece of gossip to serious national news." He sees it as "an effort, perhaps deliberate, to drive a wedge between the President and his closest foreign policy adviser in a way that could only hamper the delicate negotiations on Vietnam then under way." [2]

---

[2] Special article by Charles Colson in *New York Times,* January 29, 1973.

That is a very serious charge, even for an administration that specializes in attacks on the media. But Colson is wide of the mark. While he is right in saying there was an effort to drive a wedge between Nixon and Kissinger, the guilty party is not the press but Nixon's close ally, President Thieu. It was he who adroitly served his own purposes by inspiring reports that Kissinger had gone beyond his instructions in making the October accord with Hanoi. The press, of course, gave wide circulation to this rumor. After all, who had better inside information than General Thieu?

Colson took special note of references to the rift made on a January 8 CBS television broadcast, and to comments reported in *Time* and *Newsweek* at about the same time. By then, however, the rumor of Mr. Nixon and Dr. Kissinger being at cross-purposes was an old story, for Thieu had begun developing the theme almost immediately after that famous October 26 briefing, in which, to Thieu's dismay, Kissinger had said that "peace is at hand."

The doubts raised about the Nixon-Kissinger relationship, Colson says, "made Mr. Kissinger's task all the more difficult." That was precisely Thieu's intention. Colson also asked the following questions: "If the North Vietnamese thought there was a split, then would it not be very much in their interest to exploit it? Would not delay in reaching a final accord be wise if, indeed, America's chief negotiator had lost the confidence of his principal? Hanoi's negotiators might well conclude that if the man with whom they were dealing was in trouble with his boss, he could be maneuvered into hasty concession." [3]

---

[3] Ibid.

Thieu could not have agreed with Colson more, for that is just the way the South Vietnamese leader cleverly played it. Colson said the White House denied a rift, which is true. It is also true that the press prominently published the denial. That did not, however, stop Thieu's campaign against Kissinger. Even after Nixon had started bombing Hanoi in late December, Thieu was saying that if he had signed what Kissinger wanted, within six months there would have been bloodshed.

In a famous interview he gave at that time, President Thieu was asked to comment on the "other major disagreement you had with Kissinger." His answer was that the political formula accepted by Kissinger in October was "a formula of coalition government that the Communists want to impose on us." Thieu also pointedly said, "There are two main points, two fundamental principles, that Dr. Kissinger was ready to accept, but which I did not accept. One is the presence of the North Vietnamese troops in South Vietnam; the other is the political formula that they want to impose on the future of South Vietnam." [4]

No complaint about Nixon, mind you, just about Kissinger. What conclusion was the press to draw from these studied remarks by a leader who was in close and secret contact with both Nixon and Kissinger, particularly at a time when Nixon, in deep seclusion, had shut off official explanation of U.S. policy on Vietnam?

Now that the cease-fire has cleared the air a bit, Kissinger's role vis-à-vis Nixon is gradually emerging. There is no evi-

---

[4] "Kissinger," interview, ed. by Oriana Fallaci, *New Republic,* December 16, 1972.

dence that Kissinger went beyond his instructions at any time. The October agreement originally had the approval of Nixon as well as his number one adviser, except that the President had second thoughts when Thieu rejected the accord. In the final showdown, however, when the renewed bombing boomeranged politically, Nixon sent Kissinger back to Paris to accept a settlement that, except for a little face-saving, is substantially the same as the one his adviser had fashioned in October. Kissinger has been handsomely vindicated.

The most notable, although least noticed, post cease-fire statement has been made by Dr. Kissinger. In his January 24 press briefing on the details of the final Washington-Hanoi accord, he candidly acknowledged that the conflict in Vietnam was a civil war. If any of our recent Presidents, including the incumbent, had been willing to make this admission, the United States would never have intervened in Vietnam in the first place. Historians have Kissinger to thank for setting the record straight on this point.

Not the least of the lessons to be learned from Vietnam is that no President is to be trusted once he has made a serious mistake and starts looking around for excuses to justify what he has done. It is hard to remember all the different reasons that have been advanced for our involvement in Vietnam. Most of them have been discredited by now, but at various times they were widely accepted by the American people who, in time of war, want to believe what the President tells them.

In the early days of our Asian intrusion, the featured fantasy was the threat of aggressive monolithic communism, with the People's Republic of China doing the bidding of

Soviet Russia. When that myth was exploded, Americans began to hear about the new "yellow peril," with an "expansionist" China supposedly ready to swallow up all of Southeast Asia. Aside from reabsorbing Tibet, which had been part of China for 300 years, Peking has not swallowed anything since it came to power 24 years ago. There are no Chinese Communist soldiers outside the borders of the People's Republic.

When former President Eisenhower was on the point of intervening militarily in Indochina in 1954, he invented the now famous "domino theory"—the idea that if the United States did not save the French from defeat at Dien Bien Phu, all the other nations in the region would fall to the Communists one by one. The funny thing is that they have all toppled, not to the Left, but to the Right.

The "domino" argument evolved into the notion that our presence was needed to save Asia for democracy and give the people of the area "self-determination." This became the most popular of all the justifications for American intervention in Vietnam. General Thieu's undisguised military dictatorship finally reduced it to absurdity.

In 1966, twelve years after the formation of the Southeast Asia Treaty Organization (SEATO), Lyndon Johnson and Dean Rusk, then secretary of state, suddenly discovered that the United States was fighting in Vietnam because, under SEATO, it had a sacred obligation to defend Saigon. This came not only as a surprise to Americans, but to other major signatories of SEATO such as Great Britain, France and Pakistan, who recognized no treaty obligation to help South Vietnam militarily. The Johnson-Rusk claim subsided when it was shown that former Secretary of State John Foster Dulles, the author of SEATO, had assured the U.S. Senate in 1954 that the treaty committed America only to "consultation" and "constitutional" processes.

Mr. Nixon and Mr. Johnson have often said they had to carry on the struggle in Vietnam because of the commitments made by Presidents Eisenhower and Kennedy. The only commitment Eisenhower made was in a letter to Ngo Dinh Diem, then the dictatorial head of South Vietnam, that promised economic aid, but only on the condition that Diem initiate democratic reforms. A few weeks before John F. Kennedy was shot, he made a similar statement, saying that in the final analysis it was up to the Diem government to defend itself. The Diem regime was so corrupt, however, that it collapsed and Diem was assassinated.

In his time, President Nixon has added some new justifications for carrying on the war. One was that U.S. withdrawal would expose South Vietnam to a massive bloodbath, with maybe half a million people being slaughtered. Not much has been heard of that lately. And then, of course, we had to "keep faith with our allies," a notion that faded after Mr. Nixon's trip to Peking. Perhaps Mr. Nixon's favorite reason was the need to maintain "world prestige." It was hard to give that one up, but there was little else to do when almost every major nation in the world condemned our recent bombing of Hanoi.

One of the most welcome aspects of the cease-fire is that it will no longer be necessary for American Presidents to invent new excuses for prolonging the war. Mr. Nixon is now content to say, every day on the hour, that we "have peace with honor." Well, why argue about it? For most Americans, it is enough to know that now at last we are out of that wretched war.

REBUTTALS

JOHN P. ROCHE

There are several problems for me in dealing with what Mr. Fritchey has said. First of all, I want to avoid what might be called ontological exploration of the question of American involvement in Asia. You know the story in the Babylonian Talmud about the two schools of rabbis that argued for 20 years the question, If God really loved man, would He have created him? [Laughter.]

How we got into Asia in the first place is something I don't want to get into in that depth. I would just suggest that both the United States and, curiously, the Soviet Union got into Asia by the back door—that is, through their concern about Europe. Our initial involvement in Indochina arose from what we saw as NATO imperatives. And, of course, the Russians, in tandem with Chou En-lai, sold Ho Chi Minh down the river in 1954 in an attempt to break up the European defense community. Anyone who thinks that we got involved in Asia to make it safe for democracy is exaggerating a bit.

I once asked the late Dean Acheson why we reacted as we did in Korea. After all, I said, Korea does not seem that important strategically. He replied that it didn't have anything to do with Korea, that it was NATO. American commitments are fungible, he said. In other words, if you let this happen in Asia, what's going to happen in Europe? What's going to be the European response to our North Atlantic treaty commitments?

Now what is the major difference between 1968 and 1973? I do not suggest that the Thieu government is going to become the Southeast Asian equivalent of the Massachusetts town meeting. I do suggest, however, that in 1968 we were losing the war. I sat in the White House and kept saying, We are losing, we are losing. The reason we were losing was very simple—we weren't training the South Vietnamese to fight the war; nor were we equipping them. The contracts that made M-16s—automatic weapons—available to the South Vietnamese army were not let until the spring of 1968, after Clark Clifford had become secretary of defense.

In the recent invasion, for example, Giap brought in T-54 tanks which were much bigger than any that we'd given the South Vietnamese to work with. The problem is that Thieu would have been mopped up if that had happened in '68 because he didn't have an army. Now, in the years since '68 that army has been trained, and I would argue that it's fought bravely and well. What we term desertion is actually, in the context of Vietnam, a curious thing. It's generally a guy who goes home for the crops and then goes back to his outfit.

With any kind of luck, and particularly with continuing great power pressure, this very fragile cease-fire arrangement has a future. But, as I say, anyone who is an optimist about the future of South Vietnam should be taken off by the little men in white suits.

CLAYTON FRITCHEY

I don't want to rebut Professor Roche, I want to compliment him. I think it is true that he was the only man in the White House in 1968 who was saying that we were losing. But as to his point about ARVN, I think that while it certainly fought, it didn't fight well enough. We can go into this more deeply as the evening proceeds.

I was struck by your saying, Professor Roche, that you believe that Kissinger went beyond his instructions. I must say I spent a considerable amount of time trying to find out the truth about this and, as I indicated in my paper, I can find no evidence whatsoever that he did go beyond his instructions.

It is true that President Thieu—and I share your view and the President's that Thieu is one of the four or five best politicians in the world—did a brilliant job after the October 26th briefing in which Kissinger said, Peace is at hand. I think Thieu, almost within 24 hours of that statement, began one of the most brilliant propaganda campaigns I've ever seen to create a division between President Nixon and his chief security adviser, Mr. Kissinger. It finally was taken up by the American press, had to be denied by the White House and is still being denied by the White House.

But so far as I can see, no one has yet shown where Kissinger went beyond his instructions during the October negotiations. It is my guess that we'll have to wait some time to get the exact truth on this. The evidence seems to point to the fact that the President and Mr. Kissinger agreed during early, middle, and late October on this accord but that, in the latter part of October, the President began having second thoughts. The man who gave him these second thoughts was the man described as one of the world's best politicians, President Thieu.

I would also like to comment for just a moment on your remarks about our bombing. I think in all fairness one should acknowledge that the argument that bombing was not really tried out in Vietnam has some merit. There is no question that the air force, in a no-holds-barred situation, could have annihilated North Vietnam. The very fact that it didn't seems to me a significant commentary on this war.

It didn't because two Presidents of the United States, Johnson and Nixon, were not ready to do this. Whether it was a matter of humaneness, of worry about what Russia and China would do, or of fear of escalating the Vietnam conflict into a third world war, they both shrank from applying air power to the fullest.

So I think the air force has a case when it argues that Vietnam was not a definitive test of what it can do.

DISCUSSION

WILLIAM SCHNEIDER, legislative assistant to James Buckley, United States Senate: My question is one of fact for Mr. Fritchey. With reference to your discussion of the South Vietnamese army's performance in the spring 1972 offensive, I wonder why you argue it didn't function effectively, especially in view of these factors:

First, there were no U.S. ground combat forces engaged in South Vietnam at the time, unlike the situation in Europe today, 28 years after the end of the conflict, where there are 188,000 U.S. ground combat forces, or in South Korea where there are 40,000. Secondly, at the time of the spring 1972 offensive, 80 percent of the close air support sorties flown within South Vietnam were flown by the South Vietnamese and not the United States. Third, the fact that the North Vietnamese attacked but did not add significantly to the territory they held within South Vietnam. Why, in view of these facts, do you argue that the ARVN functioned ineffectively?

MR. FRITCHEY: It may be that the reporting from Vietnam was incorrect, but every news agency I know of—Reuters, Agence Presse-France, AP, UPI, the *New York Times*—depicted the South Vietnamese army as in flight. It was the first time North Vietnam's forces had breached the DMZ. You know they took Quang Tri. When the President began the bombing of North Vietnam and the mining of Haiphong harbor the justification for it was to save ARVN.

Maybe ARVN didn't need to be saved but apparently the President thought it did because he threw everything he had into the struggle and took measures against Haiphong which he, like Lyndon Johnson, had previously shrunk from for fear they might escalate the war to a degree that could not be foreseen. The President also did this in the light of the fact that he was only three weeks away from going to Moscow. He took a desperate chance in the eyes of most people by mining Haiphong harbor at this time, but he thought it was necessary to do it to save ARVN.

Now if we had not thrown in everything we had, I think the general opinion today is that ARVN would have been badly defeated. You remember the pictures of the helicopters with ARVN soldiers hanging on their sleds, fighting each other to get away. You remember the pictures of roads clogged with retreating units.

Was that not the situation?

MR. SCHNEIDER: That's not my understanding. The important thing is that ARVN ultimately did not lose much territory, despite the fact that the United States did not commit any ground combat forces and did not fly the majority of close air support sorties. Your assertion seems to be contradicted by events.

MR. FRITCHEY: I was suggesting to you that according to our own figures—the President's figures, the Pentagon figures—the result of this offensive is that the North Vietnamese have at least 14 divisions and 145,000 men in the northern part of South Vietnam—and, according to President Thieu, it's over 300,000. These forces weren't there before that offensive.

WILLIAM KINTNER, Foreign Policy Research Institute: Mr. Fritchey, your statement that President Nixon took a desperate gamble in mining the Haiphong port intrigued me. I was in Moscow when the first bombing of Haiphong and Hanoi took place in response to the Easter offensive. Some Soviet experts on the United States raised a few questions about the bombing, and I said, Look, you're a great power, you should know that no U.S. President is going to walk out of Vietnam with his tail between his legs. We had a very nonpolemical discussion.

But the issue I want to raise is that almost the entire U.S. press took the line that Mr. Nixon's blockading and mining of Haiphong were precipitating the third world war. What is wrong with the American press that it doesn't understand first the power realities among the Soviet Union, the United States and China, and second the local situation in Vietnam?

MR. FRITCHEY: The press's interpretation was wrong.

DR. KINTNER: That's right. Why did they misunderstand the realities of the power relations?

MR. FRITCHEY: I don't know of any member of the press that has any pipeline into the politburo in Moscow, nor do I think there is anyone in the government who has. At least when I served in government we never did.

I think it's remarkable, and having been in Moscow yourself you'll attest to this, the way the Russians are able to keep a secret. It is a most astonishing thing.

I've known, I think, every American ambassador to Moscow since 1940 and I must have known 30 or 40 American reporters who have served there. I have put the same question to everyone: Have you ever gotten a secret out of the politburo in the Kremlin? The answer is always no.

So, in this case, even the President of the United States, had to guess—to make a subjective judgment as to how the Russians would react. We must acknowledge that it was a triumph for him. There's no question about it. He took what seemed like a very serious gamble, as you know. I don't think that's any secret. He was not encouraged to do this by anybody in his own administration including those in the Pentagon, but he did it anyway and he got away with it.

PROFESSOR ROCHE: There are two questions here. You raised one about the performance of ARVN. There is a very interesting picture that appeared in the papers showing an ARVN division going down Route One obviously in terrible shape. It was that lousy Third Division, as I recall, which was trapped outside Quang Tri. But there's a bigger picture that shows the South Vietnamese marines going up the other way and yelling at those Third Division guys. What was interesting was that the first picture appeared in most places, the second appeared in very few.

The North Vietnamese really threw everything they had into that assault. There is very good reason to believe, in fact, that at that point the Chinese Communists simply signed off on North Vietnam on the grounds that it was insane. One of the things we forget is that the Chinese Communists drew a very interesting lesson from Korea: don't ever get into a land war in Asia with the United States, at least in a conventional war sense. [Laughter.] The Chinese had almost a *million* fatalities in that war.

When Giap launched this conventional invasion, a top Chinese Communist official is said to have snorted, "The trouble with Giap is that he has a Dien Bien Phu complex."

Peking's leaders decided that these people were simply insane. They wanted them to go back to Phase Two guerrilla operations at the battalion level and then fan out through the countryside.

Now on the question of the mining of Haiphong, I was in California the day that occurred. I can't speak for the whole press corps but I made a speech that night and somebody asked me what I thought the Russians were going to do. I said, I suspect they'll check with Lloyd's of London on the insurance rates because, with the mining, the insurance rates will probably go up. Given the fact that the Soviet Union now depends on the United States to feed its population, among other things, I didn't see that this was a terribly risky operation.

Which was very different, by the way, from what the situation might have been had the mining been done in '65 or in '66 or in '67. The fact that Mr. Nixon could do this and get away with it indicated the tremendous changes that had taken place in the international situation over the preceding decade.

DR. KINTNER: And a different strategic situation.

PROFESSOR ROCHE: Absolutely. Absolutely.

EDGAR L. PRINA, Copley News Services: I'd like to ask both Mr. Fritchey and Professor Roche whether it would have made any difference if the President of the United States had ordered the mining and the stronger bombing in late '68 or '69 when we had a half million troops in Vietnam? Would that have accelerated the end of the war and brought peace more rapidly?

PROFESSOR ROCHE: The problem in '68 and '69 and '70 was that there was no ARVN as an army. As I suggested in my paper, I was one of the early advocates of the Viet-namization and de-Americanization of the war, and I fought along this line for a long time. The fact is that when the Americans were in Korea, the American divisions had scouts on their flanks to make sure the ROKs were still there. It took two years to train that first ROK division, the Capital Division.

What happened in Vietnam was that under what I call the McNamara shortcut—the notion that we could run a cut-rate war without training the Vietnamese—nobody did anything about training the South Vietnamese.

Between 1968 when Clark Clifford really began to move in the direction of Vietnamization and 1972, the army was trained. Mr. Clifford started it. He became secretary of defense on March 1, 1968 and the contracts for the M-16s for ARVN, for example, were let in April or May. Up to that point the South Vietnamese didn't have automatic weapons. They just had Garands and other miscellaneous leftover stuff. The crucial fact is that there would have been a military vacuum in Vietnam if the Americans had left at that point.

MR. PRINA: My question was this: We had half a million American troops in Vietnam. With that force, plus the mining and the bombing and shutting off of Sihanouk-ville, could we have achieved peace more rapidly?

MR. FRITCHEY: Your question is really: Could we have won if we had turned the heat on them? Is that what you're saying?

MR. PRINA: That's right.

MR. FRITCHEY: The answer, I think, is absolutely yes.

The idea that the United States could be defeated anywhere in the world, let alone in South Vietnam, a small country of only 17 million people, is absurd. The United States could have won the war at any time, whether by bombing, invasion or other means. There's no question about it.

ROBERT GORALSKI, moderator of the debate: Mr. Prina, did you mean winning the peace or winning the war? Why couldn't we have won the peace if not the war in '68? Isn't that your question?

MR. PRINA: I wasn't suggesting that we were going to be defeated. I was wondering whether we couldn't have gotten a settlement in 1968 something like the one we have now.

MR. FRITCHEY: I would like to go on with the military aspects of the war because that's how you get peace—by proving that you can apply the pressure necessary to get it. There's no question that the United States could have invaded North Vietnam, could have flattened it so that nobody would have recognized it.

MR. PRINA: I wasn't suggesting that an invasion was needed—but rather just fighting it as we finally did.

MR. FRITCHEY: We are talking about the various possibilities. We didn't mine Haiphong four years ago. We could have.

MR. PRINA: Why didn't we?

MR. FRITCHEY: Now you've come to the critical question.

PROFESSOR ROCHE: At the risk of repeating myself may I take the liberty of mentioning again the memorandum I wrote President Johnson on May 1, 1967. I pointed out that a simple solution to the war in Vietnam would be destroy the enemy—and the military could do a very good job of it, if you turned it loose, doubled or tripled our troop commitments, authorized the use of nuclear weapons and so forth. In essence, the military is like the doctor who has a cure for pneumonia but not for the common cold. Therefore, he has a vested interest in the patient getting pneumonia.

What I'm saying is that there was a basic reluctance on the part of our military to go along with the limited war strategy. The question you asked really is this: Was the strategy of limited war a good one or not? All I can say is that I supported it completely, just as I opposed the invasion of the North and similar proposals, because I was convinced at the time, in 1965 and so on, that there were great imponderables in the world situation that could lead to all kinds of happenings. There was a risk of Chinese intervention, for example.

MR. PRINA: Professor, it's not just a question of limited war; it's a question of gradual application of power. That's the key I think, not the fact that the use of military strength is limited. It's been limited all along. We've never used nuclear weapons and we've never invaded the North. But the problem was the gradual application, which made the war limited in everything but duration.

PROFESSOR ROCHE: Let's go back to the hard facts. The maximum number of maneuver battalions that we ever had in Vietnam was 105. Now how many combat troops did that add up to? We had an immense military establishment. For God's sake, the PX at Cholon was the size of Macy's. But we didn't have that many combat troops and those we had were fighting essentially on the perimeter of the population. I don't think at that point any combination of American combat troops and air power could have done the job.

MODERATOR GORALSKI: I think neither of you has really answered Mr. Prina's question. Why didn't we do in '68 what was done in '72, that is, massively bomb the North Vietnamese and mine Haiphong harbor with an interdiction campaign. Would that have ended the war in '68?

PROFESSOR ROCHE: There's an old Gaelic proverb. If your bubba had roller skates she'd be a trolley car. [Laughter.]

MR. FRITCHEY: It seems to me that we can agree that the United States had the power to win this war or get whatever agreement it wanted at any time if it was willing to turn on the maximum heat. We chose not to do this.

Now your question is—it's the critical one—Why did we choose not to do it? The answer, it seems to me, is not difficult to see—the government did not have the stomach for it, nor did the American people.

Let me quote from Mr. Kissinger's January 24th briefing. It explains, I think, better than anything else I've seen, why we were so uncomfortable and so uneasy about applying the pressures necessary to win. In that briefing on the new peace agreement Kissinger was asked, "Who is the legitimate government of South Vietnam?" His answer was, "This is what the civil war has been all about."

There, for the first time, a principal, official spokesman of the government acknowledged that this is a civil war. It has been this uncomfortable realization that has prevented every President, every secretary of defense from going all-out to win this war. No President has been willing, either for humane reasons or for the fear of triggering an escalation, to do what Mr. Nixon finally did.

MR. PRINA: Couldn't that statement about civil war be self-serving though, since we had to agree to allow 145,000 North Viets to remain below the DMZ?

MR. FRITCHEY: I didn't understand it that way, but I'd be glad to go back and get the whole text out. It may very well be.

If it means what it seems to say—that this is a civil war, as many of us have always believed—it shows why we have acted as we have. If we had acknowledged some years ago that it was a civil war, we would never have intervened in the first place.

PROFESSOR ROCHE: Wait a minute now. If the East Germans invaded West Germany, are you saying this would be a civil war?

MR. FRITCHEY: I would say that's a very different question.

PROFESSOR ROCHE: No, no. I'm sorry, I don't agree.

MR. FRITCHEY: A *very* different question. Let me give you my analogy for it. We had a civil war in the United States about 100 years ago. It was not too different in that it was the North against the South, in that the issue was ideological—slavery in one case, communism in the other—in that a North wanted to impose its way of life on a South (or vice versa, if you prefer). Fortunately, we did not have any major powers intervening seriously in our civil war. If we had we would not have liked it. Yet we chose to intervene in an almost identical situation in South Vietnam.

Up until 1954 no one had ever heard the terms North Vietnam and South Vietnam. We thought of it as Vietnam for 2,000 or 3,000 years, a country of three regions—Tonkin in the north, Annam in the middle, Cochin in the south. No one had heard of a North or a South Vietnam until the wizards at the 1954 Geneva Conference dreamed up a temporary military demarcation line at the 17th parallel. Yet today, in the new agreement, it's still referred to as the provisional military line of the 17th parallel. There is no real North and South.

We fought our civil war, as Lincoln said time and again, for union. The Vietnamese are doing the same thing. And who knows what the outcome is going to be? I don't think there's anyone here tonight who can say what that outcome is going to be or how long Thieu will last. Fortunately we're going to be out of the situation. No one in the United States is going to care very much longer what the resolution of the situation in Vietnam finally is. It will no longer push us into actions which will divide our own country and jeopardize our position in the Far East.

PROFESSOR ROCHE: I don't want to get involved in historical detail, but I think Vietnam has been unified for something like only 40 years in the last 2,000. And that may be an exaggeration.

My second point is that if there weren't two Vietnams then why did the Russians nominate both of them for membership in the United Nations in 1957 and again in '58? Surely the Soviet Union wasn't about to nominate a nonstate to membership in the United Nations.

MR. FRITCHEY: They do this consistently, with North and South Korea and East and West Germany. You know their ploy as well as I do, John.

PROFESSOR ROCHE: Certainly. What I'm suggesting is that the analogy between East Germany and West Germany is precisely applicable to Vietnam.

MR. FRITCHEY: Well, in any case, whether or not it's a civil war, the President's official spokesman has described it as such and, in so doing, he has destroyed the principal argument we have used to justify this war for the last 10 years.

In my formal paper I discussed the various justifications American Presidents have used for continuing the war. Let me add another. We have heard we must prevent a blood-bath, that 500,000 people will be killed if we leave. I doubt very much that this will occur. The President has said over 500,000 people were killed in North Vietnam. As you know, there is no substance to this whatsoever. The White House finally had to admit about a month or six weeks ago that it got this information from a book written by a man named Hoang Van Chi, an exile from North Vietnam who, when exposed by Professor Gareth Porter, had to say publicly that it was a guess.

It's not much of a testimony to my profession that nobody at the White House asked the President at the time where he had gotten his figure. It took a professor from Cornell named Gareth Porter to go to the White House and ask for the source. That's how he found out that the National Security Council had gotten the figure from Hoang Van Chi.

PROFESSOR ROCHE: May I just make one point here? Dean Rusk never used the term yellow peril.

MR. STANLEY SIENKEIWICZ, Senator Schweiker's staff: One contemporary theory of international relations is that we should maintain a presence in Southeast Asia in order to deal effectively with the Soviet Union and China. I would like both speakers to comment briefly on this, and to hear their ideas on what lessons we should take from our Vietnam experience with regard to our role in Southeast Asia over the next few years.

MR. FRITCHEY: Well, while John is thinking, I will be glad to give you my answer.

I think we ought to do what President Nixon is doing: remove our presence from mainland Asia and reassert our traditional dominance of the Pacific and the littoral of Asia.

MR. SIENKEIWICZ: Would that mean a substantial B-52 force in Thailand, sir, or would we pull it back somewhere?

MR. FRITCHEY: I don't think we need it in Thailand.

PROFESSOR ROCHE: One of the problems with trying to call shots in this kind of situation is that the variables change so fast. We are all talking now in the context of 1973. Just recently, in the Australian general election, the Pentagon Papers were featured as indicating that Australia had been tricked into a commitment in Vietnam by the insidious Americans. The Labor party used this argument, though I don't think it changed many votes. Basically, Labor won on economic issues.

But what actually happened is very interesting. In 1965, a madman named Sukarno was loose in Indonesia. He had just gotten a common border with the Australians in New Guinea through the Bobby Kennedy-Sukarno deal which gave Dutch New Guinea to Sukarno, though his claim to it was about as good as mine. The Australians were looking right across the Torres Straits and the Sea of Timor. Sukarno's troops were engaged in confrontation with the Malaysians. And the Australians began to feel very lonely out there.

They entered one of Mr. Dulles's erector set pacts, the ANZUS pact. (Dulles used to run around the world with erector sets.) So when the Vietnam thing began to blow up, the Australians jumped in. They were making a down payment on an American commitment to aid Australia in the event that Sukarno started trouble.

Now Sukarno is gone, and Suharto and his crowd are minding their own business. Everybody has forgotten what the world was like in '65.

The same thing was true in another case. What was the big event in Asia in the early '60s? It was the Chinese invasion of India. That got the Indian representative on the International Control Commission to change his approach and take off the blinders concerning Vietnam, which was quite a trick. But who remembers the Chinese invasion of India in 1962 as an indication that something was going on there that we should be worried about?

Now this is why, to come back to your point, the first thing that I would anticipate in Asia in the upcoming decade is the revival of a greater East Asian Coprosperity Sphere— that is to say, a Chinese-Japanese linkage. But this time, instead of the Japanese running the store, it would be a combination in which the Japanese (who have all those yen piled up in places) would give the Chinese development loans to aid the Chinese economy, which today has a GNP roughly equal to that of Italy.

I think the Russians are scared to death of this, and for very good reasons. A Chinese-Japanese combo, would be,

I believe, the most momentous thing that could occur. And there are various interesting indications that this may be happening. For example, before World War II, when the Japanese had a puppet regime headed by Henry Pu Yi running Manchuria, a Japanese economist was the top economic operator there. Recently that economist was in Peking for six months.

MR. SIENKEIWICZ: Won't we be rebuilding Southeast Asia in order to keep a finger in that pie?

PROFESSOR ROCHE: The Japanese are probably capable of rebuilding a lot of Southeast Asia without our doing much. But I certainly believe in economic assistance.

GEORGE WILL, *National Review:* I would like to meander back to the topic for a second, which is—[Laughter] —why we ended the war when we did and as we did. There seems to be some feeling, particularly on Mr. Fritchey's part, that the nature of the ending is related in some way to the nature of the commitment. You also raised the question of the bloodbath, and of our implicit commitment to prevent it, if indeed it is likely.

I would like to ask you two questions. First, there are, are there not, commitments of deed as well as letter? And would not our connivance in the execution of Mr. Diem constitute a commitment of deed? Didn't we become deeply involved in the ultimate fate of a country by helping to depose its government?

Second, with regard to the bloodbath, if indeed a bloodbath were likely, do you think we would have a commitment to be specially concerned about the ending of the war? You say that Mr. Nixon based his estimate of the danger of a bloodbath on one report from one unreliable man, subsequently disproved by a Cornell professor. What inference would you draw from the events in Hue—which did seem to indicate that a bloodbath was possible?

MR. FRITCHEY: I think in the middle of a war there are atrocities committed by everybody, whether German, Russian, North Vietnamese, or American, as in Mylai. It is inevitable. These things are unfortunate, but they do occur.

In the case of the bloodbath that the President was referring to, the implication was that this purge took place in the immediate wake of the 1954 Geneva Agreement. But every study that has been made has proved that this is not the case.

There was a purge to use another term, about two years later when North Vietnam did what had been done earlier in Russia—that is, reorganize its agriculture, with inevitable suffering for the small landlords. A North Vietnamese scholar has estimated the number of those who died at around 15,000 or 16,000. This is a guess. A number of others say 24,000. I have seen another estimate of 8,000. Who knows what it really is?

PROFESSOR ROCHE: Well, Giap *allowed* to 200,000, though they may not all have been killed.

MR. FRITCHEY: Very few governments just slaughter for the fun of slaughtering. They want to resolve problems and get on with it. In my opinion, there is literally no incentive to produce a mass slaughter in South Vietnam today along the lines of what was done in Indonesia. Though it may occur.

MR. WILL: If I could just tie down the fact that 5,000 appears to be the number of people who were systematically slaughtered in Hue during the Tet occupation. Now, an extrapolation from those figures would come to something considerably more than the 15,000 you say died—not for the fun of it, no one is saying that it was for the fun of it—but for the Communists' own purposes. You're saying that was an aberration in Hue?

MR. FRITCHEY: No, no. I'm saying that the situation in the middle of a conflict is very different from the situation once you have a cease-fire, as you have now, or as we had after the 1954 Geneva Agreement. A cold-blooded purge where you murder half a million people for no particular sensible reason is very different from people getting killed at Mylai or being destroyed in attacks on Hue. That is in the middle of a war. All kinds of terrible things occur in the middle of a war. A million men died in one month at Verdun, and that seems insane now. But that is what happens in wars.

I think one must make a distinction between that and a postwar situation such as we are coming into now, or such as we had after the 1954 agreement. I think it is a legitimate distinction.

CHARLES FERRIS, Senate Democratic Policy Committee: I have a question for Professor Roche. In your opinion, first, has this country fulfilled its obligations to South Vietnam? And second, will the United States have any further obligation if after all the American troops have been removed, the South Vietnamese government falls, either by its own weight or because of cheating from the other side of the cease-fire?

PROFESSOR ROCHE: That's a very tough question to answer. In the improbable event that the Communists take power by peaceful means in South Vietnam, I would say, All right, that's the way it is—that's the name of the game. For us to go back into Vietnam in the event of a great deal of foul play seems to me basically out of the question. I don't think we would do it. My logic for this would be that we have given the Thieu government the stuff it needs to be able to defend itself, and that this fulfills our commitment. That commitment, by the way, exists in letters carved in marble—that is, in a letter from Jack Kennedy to South Vietnamese President Diem on December 15, 1961, saying flatly that we were going to stay there and that we had a commitment.

If Thieu throws it away, if the South Vietnamese are incapable of dealing with the situation—in other words, if the cease-fire works but Thieu loses anyway—I can't see the United States going back in.

Now, if you ask me how do I feel about it, that again, is a very difficult question to answer. Finally, ever since the murder of Diem—and I was anti-Diem, but also anti-coup—ever since the murder of Diem, it has seemed to me that the United States nailed its flag to the mast in Saigon. And this is the point at which it seems to me we irrevocably committed our honor, if I may use that philistine word, to the future of the South Vietnamese people.

MR. FERRIS: If we do not have an obligation, having been there for so many years, to structure some form of government acceptable to us in South Vietnam, has not the purpose of the past four years of America's participation in the violence really been just to save face? What has happened in the past four years to dissipate the obligation we had? We have redefined it apparently. But, I don't see what the redefinition is.

PROFESSOR ROCHE: It would seem to me that our obligation in legal terms, if I may stick to that for a minute, involved putting the government of South Vietnam in a position where it could float on its own bottom. How far beyond that moral commitments can go is a separate question.

For example, we have no treaty whatsoever with Israel, and yet if Israel were invaded tomorrow morning and were in danger of being destroyed, I would be for action like that [snapping fingers], because I have certain fundamental notions about this—which Henry Fairlie would undoubtedly excommunicate me for if he had the papal authority.

GENE LA ROCQUE, Center for Defense Information and United States Navy (retired): Both of you gentlemen have done an excellent job of putting Vietnam in good perspective, and I have been impressed with your prescience in looking into the future. But I wonder if we could take advantage of your knowledge and ask you each to address two specific questions. First, what did the United States gain by delaying the peace agreement from 1969 to '73? And, second, what did the United States lose by delaying that agreement from 1969 to '73?

MR. FRITCHEY: Well, it is certainly a most serious and legitimate question and it's one I, like most of my colleagues and everyone who is deeply interested in that situation, have given a lot of thought to. It would be a pity for us not to salvage some lesson from this unhappy exercise. Unfortunately, at this point I think it is impossible to give an answer that would be accepted by everybody. But that doesn't deprive us of the privilege of trying.

It is not difficult to anticipate my general answer, since I think the war has been a disaster from its beginning. The most hopeful thing, as I have said several times, is that our withdrawal seems to open up great new opportunities, and I am much more interested in discussing the opportunities I see ahead than what might have been.

But, to deal for another minute or two with your question, I don't believe anybody can prove that we could have gotten an accord in 1969 comparable to the one we now have. I think you can make a case for it. You can also make a case, as I tried to in my opening statement, that we might have been better off if we had withdrawn unilaterally in 1969 and not paid the price that we did in the succeeding four years. You can also argue that even the government of Mr. Thieu would be as well off or perhaps better off if the United States had withdrawn, even unilaterally, four years ago. But we could spend the rest of the night on this issue.

The big thing is that the President has made what I think are some very practical, realistic bets for the future. He has abandoned the notion we once had of monolithic communism, of China being a satellite of Russia, and, therefore, of a worldwide expansionist Communist movement. Whether or not he is right, that is his bet.

He has also made a bet that China as its stands today, and for the foreseeable future, is not an expansionist power. And again, I think he has a lot going for him on that, because, despite the notion cultivated assiduously in this country by the highest authority that this is so, the Chinese have not been expansionist. If you ask where they have expanded beyond their borders in the 20 or 22 years they have been in power, people say Tibet. The fact is, of course, that Tibet was a part of China for 300 years, up until a new line was drawn in 1904-1905-1906. Both Chiang Kai-shek and the Communists said hundreds of times that the first order of business upon returning to power would be to reabsorb Tibet. And Chiang Kai-shek never criticized the Communists for moving in and reabsorbing Tibet. Tibet has been a part of China much longer than Texas has been a part of the United States.

Other than that, I don't think there has been a Communist Chinese soldier outside of China except for a two-week border incident with India up in the mountains in 1962.

DR. KINTNER: There were a million in Korea.

MR. FRITCHEY: I'm coming to that.

But to finish my point about the '62 border incident, I was at the U.N. at the time and the great body of opinion there was that the Chinese were under provocation. As soon as they got an understanding on the correction of the boundary, they voluntarily withdrew. And I can assure you that there was nothing to stop them if they had wanted to keep on going.

Now, as to Korea. It was, I think, one of the great tragedies of our whole Asian policy that, after winning the Korean War, we escalated it to a point where it threatened China.

I greatly admire Mr. Truman, feel deeply loyal to him. Yet I must say that this was the beginning of his problems. He tried to apply the policy of containment, which succeeded pretty well in Europe, to China. It has been trouble ever since.

If you look back over the intelligence that was coming into the State Department in those days, and which the

205

White House saw too, you'll find plenty of advice there as to how that civil war in China was going to come out. Had we not intervened in the Chinese civil war, we would never have sent the Seventh Fleet to Formosa and we would have never gone up to the Yalu and invited the situation that finally came about. (And mind you, this is the chronology as I saw it from a position within government, where I then was.) It was during this time, during the Korean War and after, that we became deeply antagonistic to the Chinese, that we began pouring supplies into Indochina, in '52, '53, and later.

So one step led to another. But it began with our intervening in one civil war and ended with our intervening in another one. And I believe Mr. Nixon is getting us out of this situation.

PROFESSOR ROCHE: First, a comment about Korea. When the Korean War started we were probably about three or four weeks from recognizing the Chinese Communists regime. It is intriguing that Dean Acheson's famous Press Club speech—in which Acheson, following MacArthur's lead of the year before, drew the perimeter of defense and left Korea out of it—contains a very interesting discussion of the possibility of Mao Tse-tung becoming a Tito. The notion that high places in the American government have been populated by morons over the years is not necessarily correct, but, unfortunately, it has on occasion occurred.

Now, what happened when the Chinese intervened massively in Korea was that suddenly we went back into the Ice Age as far as dealing with mainland China was concerned.

Now, admiral, I would appreciate it if you would repeat your question.

206

ADMIRAL LA ROCQUE: Thank you. I think you have been very adroit all evening in avoiding the basic issue, which is, What specifically did we gain and lose by delaying the peace agreement from 1969 to 1973?

PROFESSOR ROCHE: I'm sorry. I thought I had addressed myself to that question in my earlier remarks. The difference between '69 and '73 is the difference between defeat and the possibility, not of victory in the old sense, but of a Korean stalemate solution. That is to say, in 1968 we were behind the eightball.

ADMIRAL LA ROCQUE: The trouble with that, professor, is that you also said anybody who thought this agreement was going to bring peace and harmony in South Vietnam was a candidate for the nut house.

PROFESSOR ROCHE: I said that about anyone who is an optimist about the agreement. I hope I qualified my answer sufficiently a minute ago when I said the possibility of self-determination today as distinct from the certainty of defeat in '68.

ADMIRAL LA ROCQUE: Could you be more specific in terms of this four-year period?

PROFESSOR ROCHE: I thought I had suggested that the reason for the difference between now and then is the existence of ARVN, of a South Vietnamese army which is equipped and hopefully is capable of handling its own end of the war.

ADMIRAL LA ROCQUE: You have been more specific than Mr. Fritchey. And I wonder if he might speak to that point?

MR. FRITCHEY: I don't see how I could be more specific. I have tried in seven or eight ways, as tactfully as I can, to say that I think the last four years have been a dreadful disaster and a waste and that we could have repositioned ourselves four years ago just as well as we have done now. Four years ago it might have ended with South Vietnam going Communist. For all I know, it may still end that way.

MODERATOR GORALSKI: We started the program with that question and we have ended with it. Thank you both very much, John Roche and Clayton Fritchey.

The American Enterprise Institute believes that debate is important because it frames issues and that framing issues is important because it makes citizens better informed.

Thank you and good night. [Applause.]